BLUEPRINTING

AN INQUIRY-BASED CURRICULUM

PLANNING WITH THE INQUIRY DESIGN MODEL

National Council for the Social Studies
www.socialstudies.org

co-published with

C3 TEACHERS
COLLEGE CAREER & CIVIC LIFE
www.c3teachers.org

KATHY SWAN

S.G. GRANT

JOHN LEE

First published in 2019.

This book is a co-publication of National Council for the Social Studies and C3 Teachers.

National Council for the Social Studies (NCSS) is the largest professional association in the United States devoted solely to social studies education. Founded in 1921, its mission is to provide leadership, service, and support for all social studies educators. NCSS is the publisher of the National Curriculum Standards for Social Studies and the College, Career, and Civic Life (C3) Framework for Social Studies State Standards.

C3 Teachers is a collaborative network of over 8,000 educators that aims to empower teachers as they work through the challenges and opportunities of inquiry-based instruction grounded in the College, Career, and Civic Life (C3) Framework for Social Studies State Standards. Through the network, teacher leaders share professional development ideas, resources, and online tools to support and sustain inquiry that uses the Inquiry Design Model (IDM) as its foundation.

Editorial staff on this publication: Michael Simpson, National Council for the Social Studies

Design and layout: Gene Cowan, Cowan Creative

ISBN: 978-0-87986-116-2 | Printed in the United States of America

6 5 4 3 2 1

TABLE OF CONTENTS

Acknowledgments...1

Introduction 3

    Why Another Book on the Inquiry Design Model? 4

    Structure of the Book 6

CHAPTER 1

The Foundation for Inquiry: Questions, Tasks, and Sources.......................... 9

    The Historical and Conceptual Roots of Inquiry...9

    The Why... Why Not of Inquiry...12

    The Role of Questions, Tasks, and Sources..14

    Conclusion 24

CHAPTER 2

Types of Inquiry.. 27

    But First, A Look to Picasso for Inspiration...27

    Building a Curricular House through Inquiry 29

    Note about Inquiry Types 32

    A Look Ahead.. 34

    Conclusion 35

CHAPTER 3

Structured Inquiry: Getting Started with the Blueprint 37

    IDM's Backward Design Process... 38

    Characteristics of a Structured Inquiry 40

    Anatomy of a Structured Inquiry: Can Words Lead to War?........................... 41

    Design Considerations for a Structured Blueprint 51

    Affordances and Constraints of a Structured Inquiry.................................... 57

    Conclusion 57

CHAPTER 4

Embedded Action Inquiry: Asking Problem-Based Compelling Questions........................... 59

    Civic Action 60

    Characteristics of an Embedded Action Inquiry.. 62

    Anatomy of an Embedded Action Inquiry: Does My Community Have Enough Food?............ 64

    Anatomy of an Embedded Action Inquiry: How Can I Make A Change? 71

    Design Considerations for an Embedded Action Inquiry 74

    Affordances and Constraints of an Action Inquiry..76

    Conclusion 77

CHAPTER 5

Focused Inquiry: Collapsing the Blueprint to Focus on a Disciplinary Skill or Concept.......79

Focusing on Concepts, Skills, and Sources 80

Characteristics of a Focused Inquiry 85

Anatomy of a Focused Inquiry: How Should We Remember Columbus?................87

Design Considerations for a Focused Blueprint..92

Affordances and Constraints of a Focused Inquiry..99

Conclusion 99

CHAPTER 6

Guided Inquiry: Scaffolding Student Research in an Inquiry.................... 101

Scaffolding Inquiry 102

Characteristics of a Guided Inquiry 104

Anatomy of a Guided Inquiry: How Do Children Make History?...........................105

Design Considerations for a Guided Blueprint..111

Affordances and Constraints of a Guided Inquiry..117

Conclusion 117

CHAPTER 7

Student-Directed Inquiry: Handing the Blueprint Over to Students 119

What Do We Mean by Student Agency? 120

Characteristics of a Student-Directed Inquiry 122

Anatomy of a Student-Directed Inquiry Blueprint: What Makes a Movement Successful? 123

Design Considerations for a Student-Directed Blueprint 131

Affordances and Constraints of a Student-Directed Inquiry..................................135

Conclusion 137

CHAPTER 8

Looping Inquiry...139

What Do We Mean by Looping Inquiry? 140

Looping Focused Inquiries Across a Course: An Eleventh-Grade Example............141

Looping Different Kinds of Inquiry Across a Course: A Third-Grade Example 144

Looping Inquiry Across Grade Levels: A Middle School Example 146

Design Considerations for Looping Inquiry 149

Affordances and Constraints of Looping Inquiry 150

Conclusion 151

CHAPTER 9

Assessing Inquiry 153

Why Assess? 153

The Very Real Problem of Assessment 154

Assessment System in IDM 155

Anatomy of an Assessment System 157

The Assessment System in Action 161

Affordances and Constraints of a Guided Inquiry 168

Conclusion 169

CHAPTER 10

IDM As a Way of Thinking 171

Solving Problems Through IDM Thinking 172

IDM in the Big Curriculum Picture 177

Final Thoughts 180

Conclusion 185

About the Authors 189

Acknowledgments

We would like to acknowledge the teachers who have inspired this book. They all have something in common—they lack a "satisfaction" gene. While we stand on the sidelines of their classrooms applauding and chronicling their innovations, they want more and better. They want to increase student agency, they want to tie assessment to inquiry-based curriculum and instruction, and they want everyone in their building to teach with inquiry—they simply are not satisfied with their own excellence. In her famous poem, "Extravagant Spirits," Maya Angelou wrote, "…they draw us from the safe borders and into the center of the center ring….there is no moderation in their nature." C3 teachers steal us away from complacency and continue to fuel our collaboration with their leadership, curiosity, laughter, bravery, and persistence.

We would also like to thank our families who have a few *compelling questions* of their own (e.g., When are you going to finish this book? Are you still on the phone with those two?). We know they have their own set of *tasks* that they would like us to complete and mounds of household *sources* they would like us to put away already. They share a common inquiry: When will those three have enough of inquiry? Sadly, no time soon. Regardless, we thank them for their enduring patience and support.

And, we would like to thank each other. We joke (well, Kathy does) that we are C3 married. We know each other well enough to often finish each other's sentences and to let it go when one of us is cranky and pops off at another. Our conversations still feel electric when we work together on a knotty idea and we are deeply grateful to have built an inquiry-yoked life together.

Kathy Swan

S.G. Grant

John Lee

Introduction

Inquiry is to education as liberty is to democracy—it's baked into the cake. From our initial training as educators, we are imprinted with a similar message: Inquiry-is-good. Whether our methods instructors emphasized constructivism, cited Dewey, or modeled project-based learning, educators get the memo—Inquiry is the way to teach and it is the way that students optimally learn. But what is inquiry? In your next department meeting, try asking that question and see if you get anything close to a clear, coherent, *and* common definition of inquiry. We suspect you won't. Educators can take heart though. If we were in a room full of politicians, imagine how varied the responses would be to the question, "what is liberty?"

Except inquiry should be different than liberty. While liberty speaks to a state of being or an ideal worth seeking, inquiry should be a reality that is measurable, explicit, and visible in classrooms. If we are convinced that inquiry is the way to teach and learn and we expect teachers to do it, we should be able to define inquiry and know that educators all mean the same (or a similar) thing. In other words, teachers should have a common and clear language around what inquiry is and how to do inquiry in thoughtful and practical ways.

Building a language with colleagues around inquiry is essential if we want the language to be spoken and student inquiry experiences to multiply. The publication of the *College, Career, and Civic Life (C3) Framework for Social Studies State Standards* provided a starting place for a social studies inquiry vernacular by defining the four dimensions of the Inquiry Arc and developing a specific vocabulary for the independent but inter-related parts of inquiry (e.g., compelling and supporting questions, disciplinary sources, claims and counter-claims, taking informed action).[1]

The Inquiry Design Model (IDM) expands those C3 Framework ideas by giving teachers the curricular tools to begin speaking the language of inquiry in their classrooms.[2] But languages need to be spoken with others. If a person spends six months learning to speak Italian, she wants to go to Italy and speak with Italians (and enjoy the sights, smells, and sounds of Italy!). Similarly, the language of inquiry is meant to live in individual classrooms and becomes most powerful when we can speak with colleagues within and across grade levels.

Blueprinting an Inquiry-Based Curriculum is intended for educators who want to do just that—to speak fluent inquiry across a social studies course and throughout their schools and districts. In this book, we elaborate on the ideas presented in our first two books on the Inquiry Design Model (IDM)[3] by pushing on the original model to think not just about a singular experience of inquiry, but inquiry as a routine practice in social studies classrooms. More importantly, this book honors the curricular dialects of IDM inquiry that have grown out of the experiences of teachers who have innovated with the original blueprint model and want even more from inquiry.

Why Another Book on the Inquiry Design Model?

A university colleague recently asked what was happening in our C3-IDM-social studies world. When we reported that we were finishing up another book, he seemed confused, replying, "Wait, what?! Really? Another one?" We know, we know, but yes, this is another book on IDM-flavored inquiry.

We blame the teachers! The three of us have weekly conference calls, and every time we turn to check-ins about our kids and colleagues, up pops an email from a teacher who has done something so cool, so ambitious with the blueprint that we can't help but expand our original IDM thinking. It turns out that the C3 Framework, the Inquiry Arc, and the development of our original blueprint model featuring questions, tasks, and sources were just the beginning. Teachers have taught us that those three elements of inquiry provide a foundation for all kinds of blueprint configurations and ways to think about entire curricula through the IDM.

We have had the great fortune of learning from teachers on a scale that we could have never imagined possible. While we each work with dozens of students and teachers in our classes at our universities, and that work is incredibly fulfilling and impactful, the C3 Teachers network has given us a unique and powerful opportunity to work at another level, with not just dozens, but thousands of teachers who all share a passion for inquiry and a willingness to try something new.

C3 Teachers has accelerated the C3 Framework and animated IDM in ways we could never have done on our own. C3 Teachers is a collaborative network of over 13,000 teachers sharing their approaches to using the C3 Framework and inquiry instruction in social studies. The network aims to empower teachers as they wrestle with the big ideas and instructional implications of the C3 Framework and the Inquiry Arc embedded within it. The C3

Teachers network and website (www.c3teachers.org) support teachers as they work through the challenges and opportunities of inquiry-based instruction using the Inquiry Design Model as its foundation. The network features teacher leaders, professional development materials, and online tools to support and sustain inquiry development. The overall strategy of C3 Teachers is anchored in an open-source approach to participation through sharing information and resources, while elevating the best and most effective products.

The spirit of C3 Teachers is evident in this book. The teachers in the network have inspired the variations on the blueprints that are central to the book. You'll learn more about each of these— embedding informed action, developing shorter focused inquiries, as well as guided inquiries that define opportunities for student research, and the stronger student focus in student-directed inquiry. With C3 teachers leading the way, we hope that the new blueprint models and ways of thinking about curriculum that are presented within this book will help teachers bring inquiry to the classroom.

The book introduces the idea of moving from blueprinting a single inquiry to blueprinting an entire inquiry-based curriculum. Structured Inquiry was our first blueprint design. We call it the "Coke Classic" because it presents all of the big ideas that initially grounded our thinking about inquiry. Questions, tasks and sources have endured as central to IDM, regardless of blueprint type. Whether we design a one-calorie blueprint or add some cherry flavor to it, we always return to the structured blueprint as our starting place to teach about inquiry.

But over the past year, we have developed four additional inquiry types for a total of five different kinds of blueprints: structured, embedded action, focused, guided, and student-directed. And we use these types to begin thinking about the inquiry experience across a course of study. We now talk about a curricular inquiry "loop" that helps teachers repeat and reinforce important content knowledge and skills essential to a rigorous and meaningful social studies education.[4]

Once teachers in a department or school collectively begin to loop inquiry, it opens up all sorts of possibilities to improve the perception of social studies by students, parents, administrators, and teacher colleagues in ways that make it more coherent, engaging, and ambitious.

Structure of the Book

We organized this book around the metaphor of a house. We begin with the foundation, which features inquiry's essential elements—questions, tasks, and sources—in Chapter 1. We have written about these three foundational elements in our earlier books.[5] In this chapter, we take a fresh look at questions, tasks, and sources as we position them as the base for an inquiry-driven curriculum.

On top of these foundations, in Chapter 2, we begin planning out our curricular house using the five types of blueprints that provide space for different kinds of rooms in the house—focused, structured, embedded action, guided, and student-directed. Each blueprint reflects variation in the role of teachers in developing the various elements and in students' experiences within the inquiry.

In Chapters 3-7, we explore each blueprint type beginning with the "Coke Classic" or structured inquiry blueprint in Chapter 3. From there, we collapse the blueprint by embedding the Taking Informed Action sequence into the formative work of the blueprint (Chapter 4) and then shrink the formative work to zoom in on a particular concept and/or skill in a focused inquiry (Chapter 5). In Chapter 6, we turn our attention to guided inquiry and how a blueprint can build up students' capacity for independent research. Chapter 7 then introduces the most ambitious blueprint idea to date. In this chapter, we present the student-directed blueprint, which provides a structure for students' independent research into the questions, tasks, and sources that make up any inquiry.

For each blueprint type and within each of these chapters, we foreground an important concept that helped inspire the blueprint or chapter. For example, in Chapter 7, we discuss student agency and how that notion is elevated in a student-directed blueprint. It is important to note that inquiry-based practice, regardless of blueprint type, offers a high-agency learning environment for students. As you read through each chapter, know that the idea elevated for that particular blueprint is also present in the other types. Additionally, we enumerate the affordances and constraints of each blueprint type so as to acknowledge that instructional choices are full of trade-offs. And, in each of the chapters, we rely upon elementary, middle, and high school blueprint examples so that we show what these ideas look like across grade levels.

In Chapter 8, we suggest that the roof of a curricular house is constructed when teachers start to sequence blueprints in such a way that they become a coherent course of study. The roof, or a teacher's approach to building an inquiry-based curriculum, ultimately holds the house together. In this chapter, we examine the concept of looping or repeating inquiry experiences across a course (a horizontal loop) or across grade levels (a vertical loop).

With the foundations, rooms, and roof in place, we shift our attention to the assessment implications of inquiry. In Chapter 9, we explore approaches to and challenges of assessment. We highlight three experimental approaches to assessment using IDM and knowing full well that there are entire books to be written about this critical topic. We start the discussion of assessment in this chapter planting a few seeds for future work in this area.

In Chapter 10, we offer our boldest ideas to date: We argue that IDM helps us solve vexing educational problems. This problem-solving focus is driven by teachers' attention to their students' interests (questions), their understanding of pedagogy and assessment (tasks), and their knowledge of content and attention to the disciplines (sources). In this chapter, we also examine other approaches to student-centered learning and the potential for IDM to work in other school subjects.

We conclude the book with a look ahead toward the ideas that are already starting to percolate for our next book(s). Ah, yes, more books to be written about inquiry!

NOTES

1. National Council for the Social Studies (NCSS), *College, Career, and Civic Life (C3) Framework for Social Studies State Standards* (Silver Spring, MD: NCSS, 2013).

2. S.G. Grant, K. Swan and J. Lee, *Inquiry-Based Practice in Social Studies Education: The Inquiry Design Model* (New York: Routledge and C3 Teachers, 2017); K. Swan, J. Lee and S.G. Grant, *Inquiry Design Model: Building Inquiries in Social Studies* (Silver Spring, MD: National Council for the Social Studies and C3 Teachers, 2018).

3. *See note 2 above.*

4. W. Parker, "Projects as the Spine of the Course: Design for Deeper Learning," *Social Education* 82, no. 1 (January–February 2018), 45–48.

5. *See note 2 above.*

CHAPTER 1

The **Foundation** for Inquiry: Questions, Tasks, and Sources

The operating metaphor for this book is a blueprint for a house. One reason we like that image is that it suggests both a set of fixed elements and the creativity to define those elements in a range of inventive ways. Houses *can* look as if pressed out in cookie-cutter fashion, but they don't have to. The blueprints for interesting, inviting, and innovative houses can vary widely, but they invariably have foundations, rooms, and roofs. In an inquiry blueprint, the foundation is composed of questions, tasks, and sources.

We have written about these three foundational elements in a couple of earlier books.[1] In this chapter, we take a fresh look at questions, tasks, and sources as we position them as the base for an inquiry-driven curriculum.

To ground this book in general and the foundational elements in particular, we thought it would make sense to take a quick look at the historical and conceptual roots for inquiry-based teaching and learning. Those roots run deep and they invariably support the idea that all students benefit from an inquiry approach. We then turn directly to the key elements of questions, tasks, and sources and show how they matter both individually and in interaction.

The Historical and Conceptual Roots of Inquiry

The number of newly published books on inquiry might persuade the casual observer that it is a new phenomenon. It's not. Teachers of even modest experience know that the reform-minded winds that blow by their classroom doors are old winds at best. So, we make no claim to be inventing fire with the Inquiry Design Model (IDM) around which this book is constructed. We freely acknowledge our debts to a strain of educational thought and practice that preceded John Dewey but to which he gave name and purpose. You can read a more exhaustive account of inquiry-based practice in our first book.[2] In this section, we hit the highlights.

Those reform-based winds blowing through schools have carried a lot of ideas over the last 50 years. Demands for smaller class sizes, stricter dress codes and uniforms, expanded certification requirements, safer school buildings, and revamped school funding formulas have fought for attention with ideas more closely associated with the classroom lives of teachers and their students—new sets of curriculum standards, new approaches to grouping students, new ways of assessing students' work, and new strategies for engaging all learners. In and around all of these latter ideas is the notion of creating opportunities for teachers and students to push beyond traditional approaches to teaching and learning. Some have done so successfully, others have not.

One set of ideas that keeps surfacing is inquiry-based teaching and learning. First routinely proposed for science classrooms, interest in inquiry has deep roots.[3] John Dewey, who took an early and enduring interest in science education, spoke to key characteristics of what we have come to associate with inquiry-based teaching and learning—a focus on problems, the importance of subject matter, the active experience of students. As Barrow notes, Dewey believed that "problems to be studied must be related to students' experiences and within their intellectual capability; therefore, the students would be active learners in searching for answers."[4] But Dewey was a broad thinker and his attention to teaching and learning in science did not mean that his ideas were limited to that subject matter. Johnston notes that Dewey advocated inquiry as "the one sure way to both solve the problems of men and to carry out increasingly democratic living."[5]

Dewey's writings spawned a range of other thinkers to promote inquiry as means of enlivening the classroom experience of teachers and students. Science educators have done the most to translate Dewey's ideas into curriculum but, beginning with the 1960s project, *Man: A Course of Study*, social studies educators have advanced the notion that inquiry is a viable alternative to transmission approaches to teaching and learning.

Inquiry-based teaching and learning can take many forms. But as we looked at past efforts to elevate inquiry (e.g., the Amherst Project and the Harvard Social Studies Project), we kept seeing the same three elements emerge. Those elements are questions, tasks, and sources.

Regardless of the approach, inquiry-based teaching and learning is centered around a question.[6] Whether those questions are teacher developed, student developed, or cooperatively developed matters less than the idea that a question frames a unit of study or inquiry. We use the language of "framing" on purpose—a question that frames an inquiry gives the content, instruction, resources, and assessments a kind of coherence that answers the dreaded student question—"why do we have to learn this?" Different authors use different terminology for such framing questions—central, essential, big idea, compelling, inquiry-worthy. Regardless of the label, it is a question that frames an inquiry rather than a title or a topic or a chapter of a textbook. Pellegrino and Kilday argue that "learning by seeking information through questioning heightens student interest and allows for creative investigations and deep analysis."[7] Bain goes further: "Students, like historians, can use historical problems to organize data and direct their inquiries and studies. Therefore, creating and using good questions is as crucial for the teachers as it is for the researcher."[8]

Questions deserve answers. In an inquiry-based social studies curriculum, those answers take the form of a summative task in general and an evidence-based argument in particular.[9] Of course, teachers will develop a range of formative tasks within an inquiry—such tasks help teachers assess whether or not their students are making sense of the content and are mastering the necessary skills. Those formative tasks, however, are no substitute for pulling an inquiry together through a final or summative task. Teachers may want to use traditional forms such as multiple-choice and short answer tests. But a test is unlikely to give students a full-range opportunity to express their individual perspectives on the framing question. So an inquiry officially ends with students constructing an argument—a set of claims and counter-claims, all supported by evidence, that answer the framing question.

In order for students to build their curiosity about a topic, to explore the content, and to generate support for their arguments, they need access to sources—the third element of inquiry-based teaching and learning.[10] Those sources run the gamut from diaries and newspapers to artwork and artifacts and from movies and maps to documentaries and textbooks. The variety of perspectives offered is as important as the variety of types of sources. If students are going to construct rich and well-evidenced arguments, they need access to sources that speak to multiple sides of an issue. Although offering students access to a world of sources brings its own pedagogical problems (e.g., corroborating sources), the opportunities to support rich, ambitious inquiry are worth the effort.

The Why... Why Not of Inquiry

Before looking a little more deeply into the foundational nature of questions, tasks, and sources, let's take a couple of minutes to talk about the benefits of inquiry-based teaching and learning...and why it is not more widespread.

Let's start with the question of why inquiry-based teaching and learning is not the norm. The research literature suggests at least three reasons. One is that inquiry-based teaching and learning can take more time than didactic approaches.[11] Lecturing has its faults, but it is a highly efficient form of teaching. Having students work through questions, tasks, and sources simply takes more time than telling them what to know. We have heard teachers say, "I don't have time to have my students inquire; I have too much content to cover!"

A second reason that inquiry-based teaching and learning has yet to be widespread is the perception that students perform better on tests, especially standardized tests, when they are taught in a more traditional fashion.[12] Although there is no research evidence to support it, the common-sense notion that students do well on fact-based tests if they receive fact-centric instruction seems to ring true and proves difficult to dislodge.

Maybe the most salient reason for the continuance of traditional instructional practices is that few teachers learned social studies through inquiry-based approaches. Researchers concur—we tend to teach as we were taught.[13] Inquiry-based teaching and learning ask teachers to rethink their roles, their students' roles, and the nature of the classroom experience.[14] Teachers can do this rethinking, but we understand that it can seem like a big ask.

These challenges to inquiry-based teaching and learning are not insignificant. We understand that standard approaches have served many students well. But they have not served all students. Our experience over the last several years confirms what the research says: Students flourish when offered inquiry-based experiences.[15] And when we say all, that's what we mean—secondary *and* elementary, academically strong *and* academically challenged students. We understand that many teachers think inquiry ought to be reserved for older and more talented students. It is a more ambitious approach to teaching and learning and it makes a certain amount of sense that the masses of students may not be able to discuss ideas in depth or to make and support arguments. But students can and do rise to the occasion. They need their teachers' guidance and support, but they will rise.[16] As Smith and Niemi note, "in history as well as elsewhere, active involvement promotes student achievement."[17]

Although we might cite any number of studies to show that students can do the kind of reading and writing required in an inquiry-based classroom, a quick review of a study that looks at both skills should suffice. In a naturalistic setting, Susan de la Paz and Mark Felton conducted an experiment to test the effect of teaching an integrated set of disciplinary reading and writing strategies on low and average-ability high school students.[18] The reading strategies helped students consider the author, understand the source, critique the source, and create a more focused understanding. The writing strategies followed the STOP mnemonic: suspend judgment, take a side, organize ideas, and plan the piece of writing. The teachers who taught about and modeled these strategies were the students' regular classroom instructors.

During the study, students read a range of documents related to standard U.S. history topics (e.g., the Spanish-American War, the New Deal, and World War II) and they wrote two argument-based essays. Although the comparison group outperformed the experimental group on several pre-test measures, the post-test results showed that the experimental group (the students who received the explicit strategy instruction) scored significantly higher than their peers. More specifically, the essays that the students in the experimental group wrote were significantly longer, but the differences in terms of quality were even starker. In short, the essays of the students in the experimental group:

- Reflected significantly greater historical accuracy;

- Were significantly more persuasive;

- Demonstrated claims and rebuttals that were significantly more elaborated.

Argument-based essays are not the only way to assess students' knowledge and skills. But because they demand evidence of both reading and writing abilities, they offer a useful proxy for what students know and can do. In this case, the low to average-ability high school students who were taught reading and writing strategies clearly outperformed their peers. In some ways, that result should offer no surprise. But what it says is critical—the more ambitious teaching and learning expected in an inquiry classroom *can* occur if teachers bring their pedagogical expertise to bear. Inquiry-based reading and writing are within the reach of all students. It is their teachers who will help get there.

Want more evidence? Terry and Panter, as well as Wieseman and Cadwell, demonstrate that elementary-aged students can engage in inquiry-based topics.[19] Bouck and her colleagues, as well as Ferretti and his colleagues, show that special education students can do so as well.[20] Make no mistake—students will struggle in their early efforts to read and write more ambitiously. But the research evidence is clear—inquiry-based teaching and learning works for all kids.

The Role of Questions, Tasks, and Sources

To this point, we have looked at the historical and conceptual roots of inquiry-based practice, why it has not been more widespread, and why it should be. In this section, we dive deeper into the foundational elements of teaching inquiry—questions, tasks, and sources.

QUESTIONS. It's not clear when social studies in general and history in particular became fixated on facts. Of course, facts matter. Historians, geographers, and economists use facts to bolster their arguments. But facts only matter in service of answering the questions that people pose. Social studies teachers will want their students to learn facts. And students will. But they will learn those facts and use those facts in richer and more robust ways if they are trying to answer a real or genuine question.

It is with that premise in mind that the Inquiry Design Model (IDM) uses questions to frame and scaffold an inquiry. Compelling questions address key issues and topics found in and across the academic disciplines and also in state and local standards; supporting questions provide the conceptual structure that helps students respond to the compelling question.

"Was the American Revolution revolutionary?" represents one kind of compelling question because it points students to an important topic in U.S. history. (See Figure 1) There are a lot of significant people, places, and events, but it's hard to imagine an American history course that doesn't give attention to the American Revolution. But a compelling question has to meet a second criterion to be truly *compelling*—it has to be phrased in a way that is relevant to students' lives. By relevant, we mean that the question speaks to issues about which students care. Brown and his colleagues on the Amherst project became convinced of this point: "The pursuit into the past of questions that students could see reflections of in their own lives— and questions, moreover, to which there were no easy answers— would deepen students' understanding of themselves."[21]

FIGURE 1: A BLUEPRINT FOR AN INQUIRY ON THE AMERICAN REVOLUTION

WAS THE AMERICAN REVOLUTION REVOLUTIONARY?			
C3 Framework Indicator	**D2.His.2.9-12**. Analyze change and continuity in historical eras.		
Staging the Compelling Question	Discuss the concept of "revolution."		

Supporting Question 1	Supporting Question 2	Supporting Question 3	Supporting Question 4
What were the political changes that resulted from the American Revolution?	What were the economic changes that resulted from the American Revolution?	What were the social changes that resulted from the American Revolution?	How did the lives of white, black, and native American men and women change as a result of the American Revolution?
Formative Performance Task	**Formative Performance Task**	**Formative Performance Task**	**Formative Performance Task**
Make a T-chart showing those political elements that changed or stayed the same as a result of the American Revolution.	Make a T-chart showing those economic elements that changed or stayed the same as a result of the American Revolution.	Make a T-chart showing those social elements that changed or stayed the same as a result of the American Revolution.	Make a claim with evidence about the political, economic, and social changes that one group of Americans experienced as a result of the American Revolution.
Featured Sources	**Featured Sources**	**Featured Sources**	**Featured Sources**
Source A: Excerpt of Abigail Adams' letter to John Adams (March 31, 1776)	**Source A:** Excerpt from "The Stamp Act" (March 22, 1775)	**Source A:** Excerpt from *The Radicalism of the American Revolution* by Gordon Wood	**Source A:** "Post-Revolution Social Changes"

Summative Performance Task	**ARGUMENT** Was the American Revolution revolutionary? Construct an argument (e.g., detailed outline, poster, essay) that discusses the compelling question using specific claims and relevant evidence from historical sources while acknowledging competing views.
Taking Informed Action	**UNDERSTAND** Research a proposed local or state tax.
	ASSESS Examine the advantages and disadvantages of the tax.
	ACT Write a letter to the editor that expresses support or opposition to the tax.

A compelling question, then, must have a worthwhile academic *and* student angle. The architect of an early inquiry-based curriculum, Jerome Bruner, argued that "any subject can be taught effectively in some intellectually honest form to any child at any stage of development."[22] Bruner's challenge does not mean that we have to dumb down the curriculum. In our view, it means just the opposite: Teachers and their students should engage in rich, intellectually robust material. There are plenty of worthwhile topics out there—surplus and scarcity of natural resources, power and responsibility of governments, the lasting effects of colonization. Social studies teachers and students have no deficit of content. The key is to see within that content the ideas about which teachers know their students care.

So if the question, "Was the American Revolution revolutionary?" hits the content requirement of a compelling question, does it also hit the student relevance criteria? We think so. We can easily imagine a teacher writing the question on the board and having students respond—"Of course, it was revolutionary! Why would it be called the 'American Revolution' if it wasn't revolutionary?" It may not always be a good idea to encourage our students to think that we've lost our minds, but occasionally it can play right into our hands. Teachers who follow up on the students' reactions with the question, "What makes an event revolutionary?" have got them hooked. There are all kinds of ways to tie the notion of a "revolution" or big change to students' lived experience: Just think of cell phones!

It would be lovely if compelling questions would just teach themselves...but they don't. A compelling question can set the content direction and it can promote student engagement, but it needs some structure around it to gain substance. Supporting questions help ground an inquiry by breaking the compelling question into chunks of content.

Supporting questions for a question such as "Was the American Revolution revolutionary?" could take any number of directions. Taking a political angle, a teacher might look closely at how the Revolution both preserved and promoted changes in the ways that the newly independent Americans would think about government and power. Taking a multi-disciplinary approach, another teacher might develop a series of three supporting questions—one each devoted to the ways that the Revolution did and did not promote important political, economic, and social changes. A fourth supporting question—"How did the lives of white, black, and native American men and women change as a result of the American

Revolution?"—brings the content elements of the inquiry together. Cast in this way, teachers and their students would have a thorough opportunity to examine the revolutionary nature of the Revolution from multiple angles (See Figure 1 on page 15).

Taken together, the compelling and supporting questions for an inquiry give it an initial content structure...and an opportunity for students to engage in thinking through a genuine question. But they will also need sources, all kinds of sources, to do that thinking and they'll need some tasks by which they can show their teachers how their thinking is developing.

TASKS. There are several kinds of student tasks in an inquiry. One kind of task is introductory in nature, an occasion to check students' initial ideas and to build their curiosity around the topic. Another kind of task helps students build their content knowledge and skills. And a third kind offers students a range of opportunities to demonstrate how they synthesize their new thinking.

The Staging the Compelling Question task serves the purpose of introducing the inquiry. Teachers might write the compelling question on the board and have students simply embrace it...or they might design an activity whereby students can encounter one or more of the central concepts embedded in the inquiry.

As we hinted at above, for the American Revolution inquiry, teachers might craft a staging activity around the notion of "revolution" by showing pictures of a cell phone, a political protest, and paper money, and then asking if any of those images represent a major change. From their lived experiences, students of all ages have ideas about what constitutes change and that change comes in different magnitudes. Young children may not have a very sophisticated sense of revolutionary change on a social, political, or economic scale but, like their older peers, they can use their own experiences to make sense of the construct. And from a discussion of change and revolution, teachers can gain an initial sense of what their students know and don't know and how they might need to tailor their instructional plans.

Formative performance tasks constitute a second kind of task. Here, the idea is to construct a series of activities that follow directly from the supporting questions. Supporting questions sequence the content that students need to understand in order to address the compelling question; the formative tasks help them learn that content and develop the inquiry skills necessary to communicate their emerging understandings. Formative tasks are not assigned randomly, however. Instead, the tasks are sequenced such that (a) students' content knowledge grows coherently, and (b) the skills necessary to complete the tasks grow progressively more challenging.

In the first supporting question of the American Revolution inquiry, students might be asked to make a T-chart of the political elements that changed and stayed the same as a result of the U.S. victory over Britain. Students might replicate that task over the next two supporting questions on economic and social changes associated with the Revolution. For the fourth supporting question—where students are asked to think about the effects of the Revolution on a range of groups—the task might be to make a claim with evidence that summarizes how one group of Americans' lives changed or stayed the same. The first three tasks, then, call for students to analyze and compare; the last formative task asks students to synthesize a subset of ideas.

Three other exercises give teachers and their students a range of opportunities to pull the inquiry together. The Summative Performance Task directs students to construct an evidence-based argument that answers the Compelling Question. The Summative Extension gives students an occasion in which they can represent their arguments in an alternative format. And the Taking Informed Action component offers students the prospect of doing something with the knowledge and skills they have built over the course of the inquiry.

An inquiry begins with a Compelling Question. The formal ending occurs with the Summative Performance Task in which students answer that question by developing an argument that is supported by evidence. As noted above, argumentative writing offers students a useful experience through which they can pull together all the threads of an inquiry. An argument is a series of evidence-based claims and counter claims that represent a student's stance on the topic under study. How that argument is expressed can vary considerably. The five-paragraph essay is one form, but students could present their arguments in a detailed outline, through a debate, or via a PowerPoint presentation. Because students' ideas can get jumbled in the syntax of their writing, we are advocates of the outline as the vehicle for students' arguments. If they can articulate the stance they are taking on the Compelling Questions and one to three evidence-based claims to elaborate that argument, we're satisfied. It's important to teach students how to write well, but writing is likely to go better if students have developed a solid outline first.

Because teachers may see the outline and the essay versions of an argument as separate tasks, they may want to consider the first as the Summative Performance Task and the second as the Summative Extension. Extension tasks can also take lots of other forms, however. Students might express their arguments as posters, as a Socratic dialogue, as role-playing experience, or as a Take-A-Stand exercise. The key to an extension activity is that it offers students an alternative venue in which to express their arguments. An extension also gives teachers another way to see what sense their students have made of the content and skills they have learned through the inquiry.

One last kind of summative task is the Taking Informed Action exercise. One of the standard complaints about social studies is that it is rooted outside of students' lived experiences. The Taking Informed Action task is intended to meet that criticism head-on by providing students with an opportunity to apply what they have learned in the inquiry to a current local, state, or national issue. The three parts of a Taking Informed Action sequence ask students to: (a) *understand* the issues evident from the inquiry in a larger and/ or current context, (b) *assess* the relevance and impact of the issues, and (c) *act* in ways that demonstrate agency in a real-world context. Examples of Taking Informed Action activities range from making a class presentation to creating a public service announcement to organizing a fundraising event for an issue or cause. Each of these actions offers students the chance to see how their inquiry-based work can make a difference in the world.

Reflecting back on the American Revolution example, the Summative Performance Task might ask students to construct a three-part chart detailing the political, economic, and social changes that may or may not have occurred as a result of the American Revolution. As an Extension activity, students might create political cartoons that reflect whether or not the Revolution was revolutionary. And for the Taking Informed Action sequence, students could research a proposed local or state tax (understand the issue), examine the advantages and disadvantages of the tax (assess the relevance and impact), and write a letter to the editor that expresses support or opposition to the tax (act in a real-world context).

SOURCES. In an inquiry, it is the sources that make the questions and tasks sing. Encompassing all of the things humans have made— maps, books, documentaries, political cartoons, artifacts—sources help students make sense of the questions and tasks in which they engage in an inquiry.

Sources play three roles in inquiry-based teaching and learning. First, they serve to spark students' curiosity about the topic. Reading a portion of an interview, looking at a piece of artwork or video, listening to a first-hand account—all bring the "social" to social studies. When students see sources as evidence of real human experience, they tend to get curious and curiosity breeds interest and engagement. The second role that sources play is to build students' content knowledge. Inquiry does not work if students are not learning about the people, places, events, and ideas that define human interaction. Obviously, there is a lot to learn, too much in reality, but the selection of sources for an inquiry gives students access to the content that enables them to work through an inquiry with growing confidence. And if all goes according to plan, then the third role of sources—helping students construct and support their arguments—comes into play. Of course, students are free to bring in information from sources outside of an inquiry, but the expectation is that they will draw largely from the sources provided to make their evidence-based arguments.

Handled well, source work can seem magical: Students' eyes and minds light up as they understand things about the human condition they might never have considered. But sources can present problems. One of those problems is that, other than textbooks, the vast majority of sources were created for purposes other than teaching students so they may be challenging for students to understand on an initial encounter. A second problem is that not all sources are equally valuable. The internet has opened troves of useful…and not so useful sources. Determining one from the other presents its own set of challenges to students. One last problem with sources is that they are human creations. There's nothing to be done about that—we wouldn't have sources if people didn't write, paint, video, or build them. But with any human creation comes a bias, whether it is obvious or not. So, students need to understand that no source offers "the truth" about a person, place, or event.

To respond to these problems, especially text-based source problems, we advocate three approaches to adapting sources for instructional use—excerpting, modifying, and annotating. Excerpting is the most common kind of adaptation. Here, a portion of a source is identified and pulled out for student use. The idea is to provide enough of the source so that students can make sense of it and use it for one of the purposes outlined above—without getting overwhelmed. Modifying a source is a different kind of adaptation. Students can struggle with sources from earlier time periods and from different cultures. So, the idea of modifying is to replace the most opaque language with words and terms that students understand; sources lose all their magic if students can't make sense of them. Making sense is key to source work so a third adaptation—annotating—helps students in a different way. Whether excerpted or not or modified or not, students may still struggle to understand a source without some context or background information on that source. Annotations can provide more information about a source's creator and its date, place of origin, intended audience, and purpose.

Each of these pedagogical moves seems reasonable to us, but we understand those who believe that any alteration of a source changes the source in ways that can lead students astray. We agree with the possibility. But when we weigh it against the idea that students may not understand anything about a source, we are willing to take the chance.

In constructing a blueprint, sources help glue an inquiry together. Sources are the material with which students complete their formative and summative tasks and through which they answer the compelling and supporting questions. To continue the American Revolution example, let's look at some sources. Space prevents us from talking through the sources for this inquiry, so we describe how an abbreviated set might be used.

The first Supporting Question asks students about the political changes that resulted from the American Revolution; the associated Formative Performance Task directs them to make a T-chart that shows political elements that changed or stayed the same after the Revolution. In a widely quoted portion of Abigail Adams's March 31, 1776 letter to her husband, John, she urges him to "remember the ladies" as he and his colleagues worked on a declaration of independence from Britain. Using an excerpt of this letter, when combined with other sources, should help students complete the task and answer the question. Here is the excerpt we would use:

> I long to hear that you have declared an independency. And, by the way, in the new code of laws which I suppose it will be necessary for you to make, I desire you would remember the ladies and be more generous and favorable to them than your ancestors. Do not put such unlimited power into the hands of the husbands. Remember, all men would be tyrants if they could. If particular care and attention is not paid to the ladies, we are determined to foment a rebellion, and will not hold ourselves bound by any laws in which we have no voice or representation.
> (https://www.history.com/this-day-in-history/abigail-adams-urges-husband-to-remember-the-ladies)

To respond to the second Supporting Question about the economic changes that may or may not have resulted from the Revolution and the T-chart task, students might look at a portion of the Stamp Act. Where a teacher might give her students the entirety of Abigail Adams's letter, to give them the entirety of the Stamp Act might cause its own rebellion. An excerpt that shows the first sentence of the act and some of the provisions should give students insights into the comprehensive nature of the law:

> An act for granting and applying certain stamp duties, and other duties, in the British colonies and plantations in America, towards further defraying the expences of defending, protecting, and securing the same....
>
> And for and upon every pack of playing cards, and all dice, which shall be sold or used within the said colonies and plantations, the several stamp duties following (that is to say)
>
> – For every pack of such cards, the sum of one shilling.
>
> – And for every pair of such dice, the sum of ten shillings.
>
> (http://avalon.law.yale.edu/18th_century/stamp_act_1765.asp)

Combined with other sources, students should be able to decide the extent to which the Revolution changed the economic landscape of the new country.

Moving to the social implications of the American Revolution in the third Supporting Question, we would include an excerpt from historian Gordon Wood's classic 1992 book, *The Radicalism of the American Revolution*. Although many of his peers discount the amount of social change that occurred for many new Americans, Wood argues that the Revolution initiated the path to the freedoms we now enjoy:

> ...if we measure the radicalism by the amount of social change that actually took place—by transformations in the relationships that bound people to each other—then the American Revolution was not conservative at all; on the contrary, it was as radical and as revolutionary as any in history....In our eyes the American revolutionaries appear to be absorbed in changing only their governments, not their society. But in destroying monarchy and establishing republics they were changing their society as well as their governments, and they knew it.[23]

Wood recognizes that these changes did not happen immediately after the Revolution, but he argues that they would not have occurred without the cleansing actions of the Declaration of Independence and the attendant war.

Students might be able to make and support an argument in response to the Compelling Question ("Was the American Revolution revolutionary?") at this point. But we think that adding a fourth Supporting Question adds a grace note to the inquiry. That question asks students to consider the implications for the Revolution for a range of Americans; the associated task asks them to make a claim with evidence about one group. There are a lot of Internet sources that provide a summary of the Revolution's effects. One we like is "Post-Revolution Social Changes" on the Alpha History website (https://alphahistory.com/americanrevolution/post-revolution-social-changes/). In a short, very accessible essay, the authors offer students a useful glimpse into the impact of the Revolution. The irony, of course, is that the Revolution had virtually no effect on the bulk of the population—the 85% of the population who were not white, property-owning men. Women, slaves, and native groups experienced none of the changes envisioned by the Revolution's leaders. The author maintains that, "if there were social changes then they were subtle, complex and incidental, rather than being an explicit aim of the revolution."

The luxury of being able to surround these sources with others offers opportunities to attend to two additional pedagogical goals. One is to present multiple perspectives. A key problem of standard social studies textbooks is the univocal presentation. Social studies is both interesting and challenging because there is no issue on which universal agreement exists. No teacher can present every perspective on a topic, but giving students access to and experience with different vantage points enables them to develop richer understandings and more nuanced arguments. The second instructional goal served by using multiple sources is differentiation. Generally speaking, it is not the content that creates problems for academically challenged students, it is the sources. Textbook-only courses can disadvantage students whose literacy skills may not be up to par. Employing sources that offer a range of access points to students of various abilities ensures more equal opportunities to engage deeply with the ideas under study.

In these several ways, then, sources hold their own as one of the foundational elements of inquiry-based teaching and learning. Their selection and use are not without challenges, but the rewards of putting students and ideas together through the use of sources are powerful.

Conclusion

Without doubt, inquiry-based teaching and learning asks more of teachers and students. Teachers can't simply stand and deliver; students can't simply sit and receive. Inquiry means engagement with ideas and between and among teachers and students. The research findings demonstrate that the benefits far outweigh the extra effort needed, but that's the case with anything worth doing. Teachers and students willing to invest in inquiry will face some challenges, but the questions, tasks, and sources with which they engage should help them navigate those challenges successfully.

NOTES

1. S.G. Grant, K. Swan and J. Lee, *Inquiry-Based Practice in Social Studies Education: The Inquiry Design Model* (New York: Routledge and C3 Teachers, 2017); K. Swan, J. Lee and S.G. Grant, *Inquiry Design Model: Building Inquiries in Social Studies* (Silver Spring, MD: National Council for the Social Studies and C3 Teachers, 2018).

2. S.G. Grant, K. Swan and J. Lee, *Inquiry-Based Practice in Social Studies Education: The Inquiry Design Model.*

3. L.H. Barrow, "A Brief History of Inquiry: From Dewey to Standards," *Journal of Science Teacher Education* 17, no. 3 (2006), 265-278; G. Deboer, "Historical Perspective on Inquiry Teaching in Schools," in L. Flick and N. Lederman (Eds.), *Scientific Inquiry and the Nature of Science* (New York: Springer, 2006), 17-35.

4. Barrow, 266.

5. J. Johnston, *Inquiry and Education: John Dewey and the Quest for Democracy* (Albany, NY: SUNY Press, 2006), 32.

6. R. Bain, "'They Thought the World Was Flat?' Applying the Principles of *How Students Learn* in Teaching High School History," in M. S. Donovan and J. D. Bransford (Eds.), *How Students Learn: History, Mathematics, and Science in the Classroom* (Washington, DC: National Academies Press, 2005), 179-213; S.G. Grant, "Teaching Practices in History Education," in S. Metzger and L. Harris (Eds.), *International Handbook of History Teaching and Learning* (New York: Wiley-Blackwell, 2018), 419-448; National Research Council, *Inquiry and the National Science Education Standards: A Guide for Teaching and Learning* (Washington, DC: National Academy Press, 2000).

7. See A. Pellegrino and J. Kilday, "Hidden in Plain Sight: Preservice Teachers' Orientations Toward Inquiry-Based Learning in History," *Journal of Social Studies Research* 4, no. 2 (2013), 1-26, at page 3.

8. See "'They Thought the World Was Flat?'" op. cit., 181.

9. E .J. Caron, "What Leads to the Fall of a Great Empire? Using Central Questions to Design Issues-Based History Units," *Social Studies* 96, no. 2 (2005), 51-60; S.G. Grant, "Teaching Practices in History Education," *op. cit;* C. Monte-Sano, "Qualities of Historical Writing Instruction: A Comparative Case Study of Two Teachers' Practices," *American Educational Research Journal* 45, no. 4 (2008), 1045-1079.

10. J. Lee, K. Swan, and S.G. Grant, "By Teachers, For Teachers: The New York State Toolkit and C3 Teachers," *Social Education* 79, no. 5 (2015): 325-328; C. Monte-Sano,

S. De La Paz, and M. Felton, *Reading, Thinking, and Writing About History: Teaching Argument Writing to Diverse Learners in the Common Core Classroom, Grades 6-12* (New York: Teachers College Press, 2014).

11. Pellegrino and Kilday, *op. cit.*; J. Saye and T. Brush, "Comparing Teachers' Strategies for Supporting Student Inquiry in a Problem-Based Multimedia-Enhanced History Unit" *Theory and Research in Social Education* 34, no. 2 (2006), 183-212.

12. S. G. Grant, "Teaching Practices in History Education," in S. Metzger and L. Harris (Eds.), *International Handbook of History Teaching and Learning* (New York: Wiley-Blackwell, 2018), 419-448; S.G. Grant and C. Salinas, "Assessment and Accountability in Social Studies," in L. Levstik and C. Tyson (Eds.), *Handbook of Research in Social Studies Education* (Mahwah, NJ: Lawrence Erlbaum Associates, 2008), 219-238; L. McNeil, *Contradictions of School Reform: Educational Cost of Standardized Testing* (New York: Routledge, 2000).

13. T. Hammond, "'So What?' Students' Articulation of Civic Themes in Middle-School Historical Account Projects," *Social Studies* 101, no. 2 (2010), 54-59; D. Lortie, *Schoolteacher* (Chicago: University of Chicago Press, 1975).

14. S.G. Grant, K. Swan and J. Lee, *Inquiry-Based Practice in Social Studies Education: The Inquiry Design Model, op. cit.*

15. J.M. Gradwell, "Teaching in Spite of, Rather than Because of, the Test: A Case of Ambitious History Teaching in New York State," in S. G. Grant (Ed.), *Measuring History: Cases of High-Stakes Testing across the U.S.* (Greenwich, CT: Information Age Publishing, 2006), 157-176; W. Parker, J. Lo, A. Yeo, S. Valencia, D. Nguyen, R. Abbott et al., "Beyond Breadth-Speed-Test: Toward Deeper Knowing and Engagement in an Advanced Placement Course," *American Educational Research Journal* 50, no. 6 (2013), 1424-1459.

16. J. M. Gradwell, op. cit,; S. De La Paz, "Effects of Historical Reasoning Instruction and Writing Strategy Mastery in Culturally and Academically Diverse Middle School Classrooms," *Journal of Educational Psychology* 97 (2005), 139-156; S. Olbrys, "The Deliberative Classroom: Inquiry-Based Teaching, Evaluative Questions, and Deliberation," *Social Education* 83, no, 1 (2019), 30-34.

17. J. Smith and R. Niemi, "Learning History in School: The Impact of Course Work and Instructional Practices on Achievement," *Theory and Research in Social Education* 29, no. 1 (2001), 18-42 at p. 34.

18. S. De La Paz and M. Felton, "Reading and Writing from Multiple Source Documents in History: Effects of Strategy Instruction with Low and Average High School Writers," *Journal of Educational Psychology* 35, no. 3 (2010), 174-192.

19. A. W. Terry and T. Panter, "Students Make Sure the Cherokees are Not Removed… Again: A Study of Service-Learning and Artful Learning in Teaching History," *Journal for the Education of the Gifted* 34, no. 1 (2010), 156-176; K. C. Wieseman and D. Cadwell, "Local History and Problem-Based Learning," *Social Studies and the Young Learner*, 18, no. 1 (2005), 11-14.

20. E.C. Bouck, C. M. Okolo, C. S. Englert, and A. Heutsche, "Cognitive Apprenticeship into the Discipline: Helping Students with Disabilities Think and Act like Historians," *Learning Disabilities: A Contemporary Journal* 6, no. 2 (2008), 31-40; R. Ferretti, C. MacArthur and C.M. Okolo, "Teaching for Historical Understanding in Inclusive Classrooms," *Learning Disabilities Quarterly*, 24 (2001), 59-71.

21. R. Brown, "Learning How to Learn: The Amherst Project and History Education in the Schools," *Social Studies* 87, no. 6 (1996), 267-273 at p. 272.

22. J. Bruner, *The Process of Education* (New York: Vintage, 1960), 33.

23. G. Wood, *The Radicalism of the American Revolution* (New York: Vintage, 1992), 5.

CHAPTER 2

Types of Inquiry

Teachers introduced to IDM are often relieved to learn that inquiry isn't a fuzzy ideal, but rather is a curricular device articulated with a defined vernacular—questions, tasks, and sources. It is not uncommon to hear teachers say, "Ah, now I know what inquiry looks like!" after working through their own blueprints.

Contentment does not usually last long though (teachers are persistently curious) and we have found ourselves inundated with questions that push our thinking around the blueprint. Teachers have wanted to know: How many times should I do inquiry in a year? When do students get to investigate their own questions? How can inquiry change over a year or course of study? Am I allowed to mess with/change/alter the blueprint?

These are all good and important curriculum questions. Inevitably, we have found that teachers want to move from an inquiry-based experience within a year (one blueprint) to inquiry-based experiences across a curriculum (multiple blueprints). But they are worried that there won't be enough time, that inquiry will become dull because the blueprint doesn't appear to vary, or that students never get to ask and answer their own compelling questions.

In this chapter, we begin tackling these questions by describing five different types of blueprints that build toward an inquiry-based approach to teaching and learning social studies. In doing so, we are creating additional building blocks for teachers wanting to make inquiry the norm in their classrooms.

But First, A Look to Picasso for Inspiration

We have been inspired recently by a set of eleven lithograph drawings by Pablo Picasso entitled "Bull" (1945-1946). In this series, Picasso visually dissects the figure of a bull by moving from a representative drawing to increasingly more abstract images until he whittles the bull down to its essence. (Figure 2.1 on page 28 presents a composite of these drawings.) Even as the drawings shed details

FIGURE 2.1: PICASSO'S REPRESENTATIONS OF A BULL

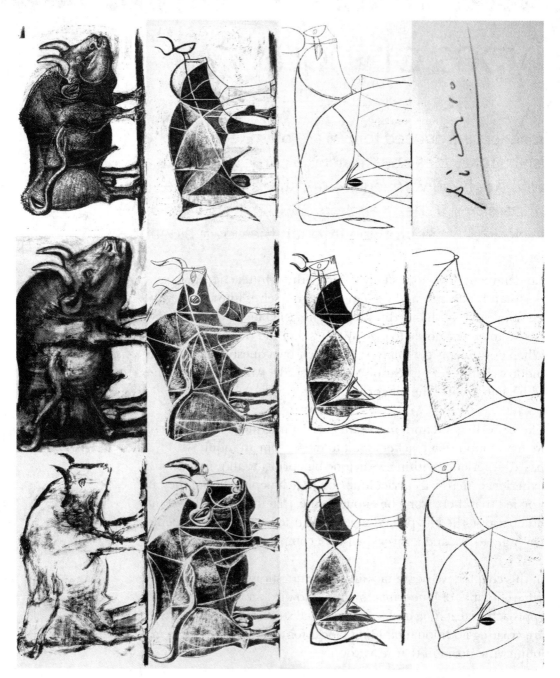

(Pablo Picasso, 1945)

such as the fur and muscles and begin to morph through Cubist and minimalist techniques, they retain the core elements of a bull and can be recognized as such.

In the process of playing with the figure and form of a bull, Picasso came to represent the bull in multiple ways. We think this same process can be applied to the IDM blueprint. Allowing the blueprint to expand or contract around the essential elements of inquiry or to be adapted and customized for student authorship provides teachers with more flexibility in implementation.

In Chapter 1 we outlined how the three elements of inquiry—questions, tasks and sources—work together within the IDM blueprint. In this chapter, we use these three elements to introduce five types of inquiry that teachers can use as the foundation for an inquiry-based curriculum.

Building a Curricular House through Inquiry

Just as Picasso played with representing a bull through his series of sketches, we have played with representing inquiry through a series of blueprints. We suggest that an inquiry-based curriculum allows students to explore the foundational elements of questions, tasks, and sources through five different types of blueprints: structured, embedded action, focused, guided, and student-directed. Taken together, these configurations help teachers build out a variety of inquiry experiences for students to span a year, rather than as an isolated unit of study. In this way, these differentiated blueprints can help to define a curriculum around inquiry and be a cohesive part of it. In the following image (See Figure 2.2 below) and in keeping with our emphasis on construction and blueprints, we represent the relationship between these inquiry elements and inquiry types through the notion of a house.

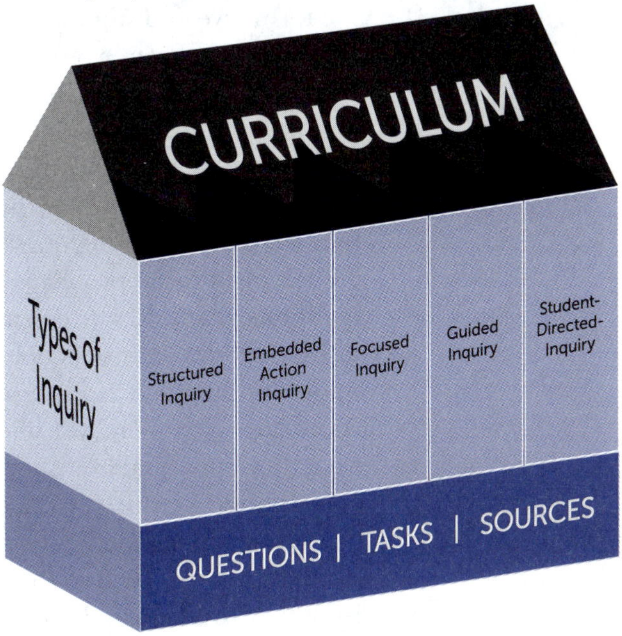

FIGURE 2.2: BUILDING A CURRICULAR HOUSE THROUGH INQUIRY

CURRICULUM

Types of Inquiry

Structured Inquiry | Embedded Action Inquiry | Focused Inquiry | Guided Inquiry | Student-Directed-Inquiry

QUESTIONS | TASKS | SOURCES

Foundation

As we described in Chapter 1, the foundation of the house is comprised of inquiry's essential elements: questions, tasks, and sources. All inquiry blueprints have a compelling question as a starting place and supporting questions to scaffold the content of the inquiry. All inquiry blueprints have formative and summative tasks, which enable students to practice and demonstrate disciplinary and civic skills. And, last but not least, all inquiries ask students to use disciplinary sources as the building blocks of knowledge within an inquiry. These three components–questions, tasks, and sources—are both elemental and interdependent and, as such, are always present in an inquiry.

Rooms

With questions, tasks, and sources as the foundation for the house, we offer five different rooms or types of inquiry in the IDM Curriculum House:

- **STRUCTURED INQUIRY** is what we like to call the "Coke Classic" or standard blueprint about which we have written extensively.[1] In this type of inquiry, teachers develop a compelling question along with three to four supporting questions to guide the investigation. Students work through corresponding formative performance tasks and a summative argument task, an extension, and/or an informed action opportunity. Teachers select a series of disciplinary sources (typically 3-4 per supporting question) that allow students to explore the supporting question and complete the formative and summative tasks. We suggest that this type of inquiry takes three to ten instructional days or class periods and is developed by the teacher.

- **EMBEDDED ACTION INQUIRY** allows students to practice taking informed action as part of the academic inquiry. In this kind of inquiry, the compelling question is crafted so that students are addressing a social problem. The formative work (i.e., supporting questions, featured sources, and formative performance tasks) provides an instructional space so that students are understanding and assessing the social problem. Then, the summative argument task allows students to demonstrate what they know and how they might address the problem in a contemporary fashion. We suggest that this type of inquiry takes five to ten instructional days or class periods and is developed primarily by the teacher, although the students determine the issue they research and the action they take.

- **FOCUSED INQUIRY** allows teachers to collapse the inquiry experience into a one-to-two day lesson.[2] In this blueprint, teachers develop a compelling question, but one that tends to be narrower in scope and, as such, necessitates only one to two supporting questions, which saves instructional time. The corresponding formative performance tasks are fewer, the summative argument task collapses to a single claim and/or counterclaim, and the end of the blueprint features either an extension or action opportunity, but not both. Lastly, teachers typically select fewer sources for students to explore, thereby further contracting the instructional time. A focused blueprint allows teachers to zoom in on a particular skill or piece of content. We suggest that this type of inquiry takes one to two instructional days or class periods and is developed by the teacher.

- **GUIDED INQUIRY** provides students with an opportunity to become more independent within a teacher-developed inquiry. In these blueprints, teachers construct the compelling and supporting questions as well as the corresponding formative and summative tasks. But, they craft at least one independent research opportunity within the formative work. Within the research experience, students might be asked to find the sources that would help answer the supporting question. Because of this additional research time, this type of inquiry may take a bit longer than a structured inquiry. We suggest that teachers plan for five to ten instructional days or class periods.

- **STUDENT-DIRECTED INQUIRY** occurs when students take on the development of the blueprint by defining the compelling and supporting questions, the formative and summative performance tasks, and the disciplinary sources for their inquiry. In this type of inquiry, teachers act in an advisory capacity nudging students' thinking about a topic, offering guidance about their investigative paths, and providing assistance in locating sources for their inquiries. Because students are working more independently around their own questions, tasks, and sources, we anticipate that this type of inquiry may take a while and suggest a two-week window of instructional time.

These descriptions of each type of inquiry are intended to be a short introduction so that our inquiry curriculum house makes sense. In the subsequent chapters in the book, we deconstruct each of these blueprints in greater detail providing multiple examples of each plan at representative grade levels—elementary, middle, and high school.

Roof

As teachers plan for these different types of blueprints over a course, a curriculum or roof emerges on our inquiry house. In the *College, Career, and Civic Life (C3) Framework for State Social Studies Standards*, we defined an Inquiry Arc that helps students, "ask good questions and develop robust investigations into them; consider possible solutions and consequences; separate evidence-based claims from parochial ones; and communicate and act upon what they learn."[3] But we didn't stop there. We assert that students must be given opportunities to take on the inquiry reins:

> And most importantly, students must possess the capability and commitment to repeat that process as long as is necessary...in order to traverse successfully the worlds of college, career, and civic life.[4]

As questions, tasks, and sources become the foundation of the curricular house and we populate the house with rooms representing different inquiry types, we become more cohesive and intentional about the larger social studies curriculum. That is, instead of a shed outside the house where students infrequently gather tools, inquiry becomes essential for holding up the curriculum.

This house metaphor has helped us break out of the initial blueprint box to include other types of inquiry that help animate the aims of the C3 Framework. In the following table, we distinguish the five types of inquiry as they relate to the foundational elements of inquiry (Questions, Tasks, Sources) and two curriculum variables, agency and time. (See Table 2.1.)

Note about Inquiry Types

As we have in previous books, we add a disclaimer: We are sure that there are more than five types of inquiry out there, and as such, we know that there are exponential ways to alter a blueprint. We trust teachers' intuitions, knowledge and experiences and offer these five pathways as a starting place for teachers who are thinking about using a blueprint to differentiate the inquiry experiences of their students.

An additional question raised by teachers is whether we intend the curriculum house diagram to suggest a pecking order with student-directed inquiry representing the highest form of inquiry. We hedge a bit on that question as we see the unique value of each

TABLE 2.1: TYPES OF INQUIRY

	TYPES OF INQUIRY				
	Focused Inquiry	**Structured Inquiry**	**Embedded Action**	**Guided Inquiry**	**Student-Directed Inquiry**
Description	The teacher develops the inquiry but focuses on a particular disciplinary skill and piece of content (e.g. causation, map work, research).	The teacher develops the blueprint to scaffold the disciplinary and civic outcomes of the inquiry.	The teacher develops the inquiry, but focuses on structuring the Taking Informed Action (understand-assess-act) sequence into the core of the blueprint.	The teacher develops the inquiry but there are dedicated spaces in the formative work for students to conduct independent research.	The student develops the blueprint on a question that he or she is interested in and plans the inquiry using the blueprint.
Example	Did the attack on Pearl Harbor unify America? *Middle School Pearl Harbor Blueprint*	Do we ever get what we need and want? *Elementary School Needs and Wants inquiry*	Why is the Affordable Care Act so controversial? *High School Public Policy Blueprint*	What made nonviolent protest effective during the civil rights movement? *High School Civil Rights Blueprint*	What makes a movement successful? *High School LGTBQ Blueprint*
Blueprint	http://www.c3teachers.org/wp-content/uploads/2016/08/TPS-Pearl-Harbor-05-16.pdf	http://www.c3teachers.org/wp-content/uploads/2015/06/NewYork_K_NeedsandWants.pdf	http://www.c3teachers.org/wp-content/uploads/2015/06/NewYork_12_ACA.pdf	http://www.c3teachers.org/wp-content/uploads/2015/09/NewYork_11_Civil_Rights.pdf	http://www.c3teachers.org/wp-content/uploads/2015/10/Kentucky-12-movement_successfull.pdf
Teacher to Student Driven	Teacher-developed	Teacher-developed	Teacher-developed	Teacher- and Student-developed	Student-developed
Questions	The teacher develops the Compelling and Supporting Questions	The teacher develops the Compelling and Supporting Questions	The teacher develops both the Compelling and Supporting Questions. The Compelling Question typically is created so that it explores a social problem.	The teacher develops the Compelling Question but 1-2 Supporting Questions are deliberately structured so students are investigating a broad question.	The student develops the Compelling and Supporting Questions with guidance from the teacher.
Tasks	The teacher develops the Summative and Formative Tasks.	The teacher develops the Summative and Formative Tasks.	The teacher develops the Summative and Formative Tasks, but some of the Formative Tasks might be structured so that students are researching a supporting question.	The teacher develops the Summative and Formative Tasks, but 1-2 Formative Tasks are structured so that students are researching a Supporting Question.	The student develops Summative and Formative Tasks with guidance from the teacher.
Sources	The teacher selects a small collection of sources.	The teacher selects sources.	The teacher selects most of the sources, but students might select some sources as they relate to the research opportunity.	The teacher selects some sources, and students select some sources as they relate to the research opportunity.	The student selects sources with guidance from the teacher.
Time	1-2 days	3-10 days	5-10 days	5-10 days	2 weeks

type of inquiry. However, all types of blueprints from structured to embedded action to focused to guided to student-directed are curricular scaffolds for students learning through inquiry.

The nature of scaffolds is that they are ultimately removed so that a structure can stand independently. The pedagogical nature of curricular scaffolds follows that same aim. As the scaffolds for questions, tasks, and sources are removed and students work more independently to create their own questions, to find their own sources, and then to create their own meaning and answers to questions, we see a dynamic and meaningful inquiry arc take shape in social studies classrooms.

A Look Ahead

The next five chapters in this book are dedicated to breaking down the structure of the five blueprints outlined above. We begin with a structured blueprint, then we turn our attention to the embedded action, focused, guided, and student-directed blueprints in subsequent chapters. In each of the five chapters, we use one educational design concept to anchor the blueprint's unique composition.

In Chapter 3, we highlight the backward design planning process as a central feature of the Inquiry Design Model. Although backward design applies to all five blueprints, we highlight the concept in this particular chapter because it seems like an important starting place in understanding the IDM approach generally, and the interaction of the blueprint components specifically.

In Chapter 4, we examine civic action as described in the C3 Framework. Taking Informed Action is an essential element of every blueprint type, but it is particularly important to the embedded action inquiry. Action often scares teachers the most. But action opportunities can occur across a long continuum of possibilities that vary greatly in location and complexity. In this chapter, we present a model for thinking about action that accommodates all kinds of classroom constraints.

In Chapter 5, we unpack a focused inquiry by zooming in on the tangled relationship among content, concepts, skills, and disciplinary sources. Focused inquiries require an additional level of clarity around the core purpose of the inquiry and it seemed appropriate to kick this chapter off with an understanding of how these elements interact within a blueprint to provide the focus of the inquiry.

In Chapter 6, we discuss the guided inquiry blueprint. As an initial starting place for this chapter, we show how the blueprint becomes a curricular scaffold for inquiry. We make the distinction between hard and soft scaffolds, and then curricular and instructional scaffolds. These distinctions exist in all blueprints, but seem particularly important here as teachers give additional attention to the instructional scaffolds present within an inquiry.

Lastly, in Chapter 7, we introduce the student-directed inquiry blueprint. In this chapter, we begin our discussion by defining student agency and its role in all blueprints. Student agency takes on an elevated importance when students develop their own questions and tasks and locate and adapt disciplinary sources for the inquiry. Again, student agency is present in all five blueprint types, but is especially pronounced in a student-directed inquiry.

Ultimately, we see these blueprints and IDM as a way of thinking about good social studies. Inquiry is not the latest fad or simply another teaching strategy. IDM allows us to incorporate the broader educational lexicon under one umbrella of meaningful and effective social studies instruction. Our hope is that like-minded educators use the IDM approach as a vehicle to teach about curricular design, assessment practices, use of disciplinary sources, civic agency, student research, argumentation, and disciplinary literacy. This book continues to connect some of these important conceptual dots, so that IDM becomes a productive way of thinking about the foundations and implications of a strong social studies education.

Conclusion

In a recent article, Walter Parker talks about inquiry experiences as the spine of the curriculum (and yes, this might be the fourth metaphor used to describe inquiry in this chapter alone!). Parker posits that when inquiry-based projects are the spine of a course, they are systematically sequenced so that they provide the substance of the course and thereby drive deeper learning. But then he zeroes in on the core role of curriculum:

> But here's the secret sauce: At the heart of deeper learning is curriculum, not instruction. Before implementing instructional strategies, teachers need to make strategic decisions about the content and skills to be learned—those that will be learned deeply, iteratively, rather than only "covered."[5]

The Inquiry Design Model aims in the same direction by organizing curriculum around the foundational elements of inquiry—questions, tasks, and sources. By collapsing or expanding and, in some cases, shifting the authorship of a blueprint, we illustrate how the IDM can operate as a curricular framework that flexes to meet the contextual needs of teachers.

In the next several chapters, we dive deeply into the five types of inquiry by providing multiple examples of each and walking through the affordances and constraints of each approach. Additionally, we provide design guidance for each type and outline how the design process might change from inquiry type to inquiry type.

NOTES

1. S.G. Grant, K. Swan and J. Lee, *Inquiry-Based Practice in Social Studies Education: The Inquiry Design Model* (New York: Routledge and C3 Teachers, 2017); K. Swan, J. Lee and S.G. Grant, *Inquiry Design Model: Building Inquiries in Social Studies* (Silver Spring, MD: National Council for the Social Studies and C3 Teachers, 2018).

2. K. Swan, J. Lee and S.G. Grant, "Questions, Tasks, Sources: Focusing on the Essence of Inquiry," *Social Education* 82, 3 (May-June 2018), 142-146.

3. National Council for the Social Studies (NCSS), *College, Career, and Civic Life (C3) Framework for Social Studies State Standards* (Silver Spring, MD: NCSS, 2013), 3.

4. *Ibid.*

5. W. Parker, "Projects as the Spine of the Course: Design for Deeper Learning," *Social Education* 82, no. 1 (January-February 2018), 45-48 at p. 48.

CHAPTER 3

Structured Inquiry: Getting Started with the Blueprint

When we first started designing and writing about the IDM, we didn't know about the Picasso etchings of the bull that we described in the last chapter. But even so, we liked the design challenge of stripping away the prescriptive details of many unit and lesson plans and finding the essence of inquiry. The one-page blueprint is an instructional map, helping teachers stay focused on the path and trusting that they know their craft and their students well enough to fill in the context for their classroom. A twenty-page map can be unwieldy if you are trying to drive. Add students to the backseat and you may be in for a wild and confusing ride. We like the idea that teachers can manage all elements of inquiry—questions, tasks, and sources—in a single page. Inquiry will never be easy, but we hope the blueprint helps teachers to manage its complexity.

In this chapter, we describe the original blueprint that we now call *structured* inquiry. We start with the backward design process that guides the three-phase blueprint development process. Then, we use a structured inquiry blueprint on the Civil War to examine its architecture of questions, tasks, and sources. We continue by looking at the design and instructional considerations for developing and teaching a structured inquiry paying close attention to issues of design alignment. We conclude the chapter by discussing the instructional affordances and constraints teachers face when employing this type of inquiry experience.

IDM's Backward Design Process

In our book, *Inquiry Design Model: Building Inquiries for Social Studies*,[1] we organize blueprint development into three design phases: Framing, Filling, and Finishing the Inquiry. These phases are broken down into 10 steps along the IDM design path. (See Figure 3.1 below.)

FIGURE 3.1: THE DESIGN PATH FOR IDM

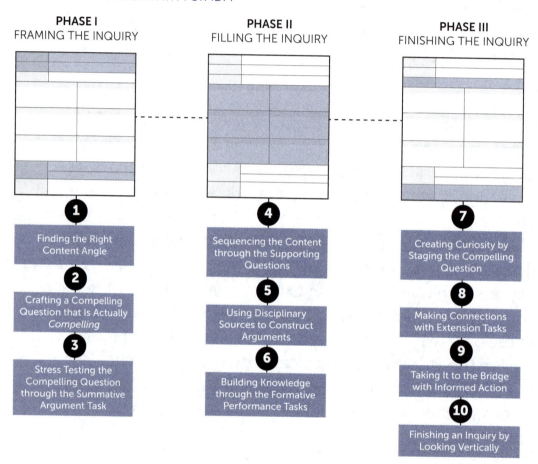

Building a blueprint begins by establishing a strong frame for the inquiry. This phase involves selecting a topic that is ripe for inquiry, mining that topic for a rich compelling question, and ensuring that the question takes students where you want them to go. In other words, we begin by identifying our instructional aims and outcomes before developing the means to get there. Many curriculum designers refer to this process as *backward mapping* or *planning*.[2] Using this type of design approach, teachers develop units by identifying their desired results, developing assessments to measure whether students were successful, and then planning the best instructional exercises to achieve the desired results.

In IDM, we embrace the practice of backward planning, but we adapt it for inquiry, which is a unique type of learning experience. In inquiry, we make several assumptions that differ from traditional unit planning and even more recent approaches such as project-based learning. In inquiry, our aim is to provide students with the space to answer a compelling question with an evidence-based argument.[3] The compelling question is rooted in local social studies standards (the aim) and is written so that it frames an argumentative task (the outcome).

Framing an inquiry, then, involves finding a juicy piece of content that allows students to authentically wrestle with a question and defend their answers with evidence. In history, this approach could mean that students are trying to understand the significance of a past event or determining how we should remember it. In civics and economics, it could be that students are trying to find a solution to a modern-day problem. In geography, students could be examining where the world is changing and how best to represent those changes through maps or geographic information systems. The curriculum design challenge is in finding the "just right" content to launch and sustain the inquiry and avoiding the dreaded content trap that we often find ourselves in when planning.

In *Phase I: Framing the Inquiry*, we work through these ideas by unpacking three elements of the blueprint: content standards, the compelling question, and the summative argument task. Each of these elements are distinct but interdependent. For example, the compelling question needs to be rooted in the standards and the summative argument task needs to be a response to the compelling question. Because of these relationships, we often use the word *alignment* to describe the quality of the relationship between blueprint elements. Does the compelling question *align* to the standards? Does the summative argument task *align* to the compelling question? If the alignment between elements is wonky, the inquiry frame will be too. And, if the frame is unstable, it is best not to build on top of it!

With a sturdy inquiry frame in place, we turn to *Phase II: Filling the Inquiry* and focus on the formative work that moves students from question to argument. In IDM, we want the supporting questions, featured sources, and formative performance tasks to sequence in a coherent way across the blueprint. In this phase, we use the word *logic* as a synonym for coherence to describe the three sequences that make up the formative work that stages across the middle section of blueprint—the *question logic*, the *source logic*, and the *task logic*. The question logic asks the designer to examine how the supporting questions house the content inherent within the compelling question and how they sequence across the blueprint. The source logic helps teachers whittle down the disciplinary sources into a collection that is both textured and manageable for students. Finally, the task logic zooms in on the formative performance tasks of the inquiry and the way in which they provide opportunities for students to practice the skills and acquire the knowledge for successful completion of the inquiry.

In *Phase III: Finishing the Inquiry,* we put the finishing touches on the blueprint by looking at three additional blueprint elements and then stepping back to examine the alignment of the blueprint as a whole. Staging the Compelling Question provides a space to kick off the compelling question and consider ways that it can become animated for students. Extension tasks breathe a second life into the idea of an evidence-based argument by providing students with opportunities to share what they have learned with others. Taking Informed Action tasks become the inquiry finale by exploring civic connections to the topic behind the compelling question.

The IDM approaches the summative tasks like runners approach a marathon—students need to train for it. By following the sound principles of backward design, IDM blueprints have a solid foundation rooted in important social studies content, sound assessment principles, and meaningful instruction.

Characteristics of a Structured Inquiry

Structured Inquiry unfolds in the blueprint format about which we have written extensively.[4] A structured inquiry blueprint is designed so that students ultimately answer a compelling question through a series of summative performance tasks. Students build up their capacity to do so by acquiring content knowledge and practicing disciplinary skills within the formative work of the inquiry. The blueprint elements of a structured inquiry are developed by the teacher, who keeps her students' interests and skill levels in mind. Teachers select a series of disciplinary sources (typically 3-4 per supporting question) that allow students to explore the supporting question and complete the formative and summative tasks. We suggest that this type of inquiry takes three to ten instructional days or class periods and is developed by the teacher. (See Table 3.1)

In the section that follows, we walk through a structured inquiry for the middle grades on the Civil War and highlight its key elements of questions, tasks, and sources. In the *Uncle Tom's Cabin* inquiry,

TABLE 3.1 ELEMENTS OF A STRUCTURED INQUIRY

STRUCTURED INQUIRY	
Description	The teacher develops the blueprint to scaffold the disciplinary and civic outcomes of the inquiry.
Role of Teacher and/or Student in Blueprint Development	Teacher developed
Questions	The teacher develops the compelling and supporting questions.
Tasks	The teacher develops summative and formative tasks.
Sources	The teacher selects sources.
Instructional Time	3-10 days

students explore how words can affect public opinion through an examination of Harriet Beecher Stowe's novel. Here, we highlight the compelling and supporting questions that frame and organize the inquiry, the assessment tasks that provide opportunities for students to demonstrate and apply their understanding, and the disciplinary sources that allow students to practice disciplinary thinking and reasoning.

Anatomy of a Structured Inquiry: Can Words Lead to War?

The *structured* inquiry blueprint is a one-page visual representation of the questions, tasks, and sources that define an inquiry. There are compelling and supporting questions, formative and summative performance tasks, and selected disciplinary sources that aid students in answering the inquiry's questions. (See Figure 3.2 on page 42). In the sections that follow, we walk through these elements in detail.

Questions

From Socrates on, the value of questions in general, and for teaching and learning in particular, has been well established. In Plato's *Protagoras*, Socrates claims, "my way toward truth is to ask the right questions." Answers are important, but a well-framed question can excite the mind and give real and genuine meaning to the study of any social issue. The IDM features compelling questions as a way to drive social studies inquiry.

The key to crafting compelling questions is hitting the sweet spot between the qualities of being intellectually rigorous and personally relevant to students. Intellectually rigorous questions reflect an enduring issue, concern, or debate in social studies and speak to the big ideas of history and the social sciences. For example, the compelling question—Can words lead to war?—asks students to

FIGURE 3.2: A STRUCTURED INQUIRY BLUEPRINT ON THE CIVIL WAR

CAN WORDS LEAD TO WAR?

New York State Social Studies Framework Key Ideas & Practices	**7.7 REFORM MOVEMENTS:** Social, political, and economic inequalities sparked various reform movements and resistance efforts. Influenced by the Second Great Awakening, New York State played a key role in major reform efforts. ☑ Gathering, Using, and Interpreting Evidence ☑ Chronological Reasoning and Causation ☑ Comparison and Contextualization
Staging the Compelling Question	Consider the power of words and examine a video of students using words to try to bring about positive change.

Supporting Question 1	Supporting Question 2	Supporting Question 3	Supporting Question 4
How did Harriet Beecher Stowe describe slavery in *Uncle Tom's Cabin*?	What led Harriet Beecher Stowe to write *Uncle Tom's Cabin*?	How did people in the North and South react to *Uncle Tom's Cabin*?	How did *Uncle Tom's Cabin* affect abolitionism?
Formative Performance Task	**Formative Performance Task**	**Formative Performance Task**	**Formative Performance Task**
Write a summary of the plot of *Uncle Tom's Cabin* that includes main ideas and supporting details from Stowe's description of slavery in the book.	List four quotes in the sources that point to Stowe's motivation and write a paragraph explaining her motivation.	Make a T-chart comparing viewpoints expressed in newspaper reviews of *Uncle Tom's Cabin* and make a claim about the differences.	Participate in a structured discussion regarding the impact *Uncle Tom's Cabin* had on abolitionism.
Featured Sources	**Featured Sources**	**Featured Sources**	**Featured Sources**
Source A: Summary of *Uncle Tom's Cabin* **Source B:** Excerpts from *Uncle Tom's Cabin* **Source C:** Illustrations from *Uncle Tom's Cabin*	**Source A:** Harriet Beecher Stowe's concluding remarks to *Uncle Tom's Cabin*. **Source B:** Letter from Harriet Beecher Stowe to Lord Thomas Denman	**Source A:** Review of *Uncle Tom's Cabin* published in the *Boston Morning Post* **Source B:** Review of *Uncle Tom's Cabin* published in the *Southern Press Review*	**Source A:** Excerpt from Charles Sumner's Senate speech **Source B:** Article by John Ball Jr. published in *The Liberator* **Source C:** Sales of *Uncle Tom's Cabin*, 1851–1853

Summative Performance Task	**ARGUMENT** Can words lead to war? Construct an argument (e.g., detailed outline, poster, essay) that discusses the impact of *Uncle Tom's Cabin* using specific claims and relevant evidence from historical sources, while acknowledging competing views.
	EXTENSION Create an educational video of the argument that responds to the compelling question "Can words lead to war?"
	UNDERSTAND Identify and describe a human rights issue that needs to be addressed (e.g., child labor, trafficking, or poverty).
Taking Informed Action	**ASSESS** Create a list of possible actions that involve words. This may include letters, editorials, social media, videos, and protests.
	ACT Choose one of the options and implement it as an individual, small group, or class project.

grapple with the power of words more generally, and the causes of the Civil War more specifically. Historians continue to tease out the profound complexity and the chains of action and reaction that caused this turning point in U.S. history. In this inquiry, students enter the ongoing historical discussion by investigating the impact of Harriet Beecher Stowe's words in her book *Uncle Tom's Cabin*.[5]

Compelling questions need to be worth investigating from an academic angle, but they also need to be worth exploring from a student angle. Recall Jerome Bruner's claim—"any subject can be taught effectively in some intellectually honest form to any child at any stage of development."[6] To take this point seriously does not mean that we have to dumb down the curriculum. In fact, it means just the opposite: Teachers should teach intellectually ambitious material. The key is to see within the ideas to be taught those elements that teachers know their students care about. It is not the case that students are uninterested in the Civil War. But it is the case that teachers need to pull relevant connections from those ideas to students' lives.

In examining the compelling question—Can words lead to war?— the student-friendly elements of the question quickly emerge. First, the question pulls on a thread that all students care about—words. Words are a powerful medium to which all students can relate: Students surely have said something they regret, repeated a word that has gotten an adult incensed, or watched as others have been hurt by an insult. Second, the question is free of jargon and is written in a way that is highly accessible for students. Students should be able to hold compelling questions in their heads in ways that are illuminating rather than merely decorative.

If compelling questions frame an inquiry, supporting questions sustain it. Supporting questions build out the compelling question by organizing and sequencing the main ideas. Supporting questions follow a content logic or progression that becomes increasingly more sophisticated over the inquiry experience. For example, in the *Uncle Tom's Cabin* inquiry, the supporting questions sequence this way:

- **SUPPORTING QUESTION 1:** How did Harriet Beecher Stowe describe slavery in *Uncle Tom's Cabin*?

- **SUPPORTING QUESTION 2:** What led Harriet Beecher Stowe to write *Uncle Tom's Cabin*?

- **SUPPORTING QUESTION 3:** How did Northerners and Southerners react to *Uncle Tom's Cabin*?

- **SUPPORTING QUESTION 4:** What was the impact of *Uncle Tom's Cabin* on abolitionism?

Taken together, the compelling question and supporting questions provide the architecture for the inquiry as they highlight the ideas and issues with which teachers and students can engage. There is no one right compelling question for a topic, nor is there only one way to construct and sequence supporting questions. The question about words and war has been vetted and found to be compelling by a range of teachers and academics, but that is not to say that others might not develop equally engaging questions on the antebellum period. Similarly, the supporting questions in this inquiry have won teachers' endorsement. Others, however, might rearrange the sequence, insert additional questions, or even substitute a whole new series. To that end, C3 Teachers publishes inquiries in Word and PDF formats so that teachers wanting to modify questions can easily do so.

Tasks

The IDM blueprint features a variety of performance tasks that provide students with opportunities for learning and teachers with opportunities to evaluate what students know and are able to do. Based on the idea that assessments serve instructional as well as evaluative purposes, blueprints feature both formative and summative performance tasks as well as extension activities, and taking informed action opportunities.

The heart of each inquiry rests between two points—the compelling question and the summative argument. What comes between (e.g., supporting questions, formative performance tasks, and sources) is designed to prepare students to move constructively between the compelling question and the summative argument. In the *Uncle Tom's Cabin* inquiry, for example, the summative performance task begins with the compelling question followed by the phrase, "construct an argument." The verb "construct" was purposefully chosen to indicate that not all arguments must take the form of an essay.

In order to make a strong argument, students must engage with content and skills throughout an inquiry. The formative performance tasks within the inquiry are designed as exercises intended to move students toward success in constructing a coherent, evidence-based argument. Although these tasks do not include all of what students might need to know, they do include the major ideas that provide a foundation for their arguments. In this way, teachers avoid "gotcha" assessments—tasks that catch students off guard or without the proper preparation for success on the summative performance task.

The formative performance tasks are framed by the supporting questions within the inquiry. In this way, the formative performance tasks and the supporting questions have a similar relationship to that of the summative argument and the compelling question. Moreover, the formative performance tasks increase in complexity so that students can build and practice the skills of evidence-based claim making.

In the *Uncle Tom's Cabin* inquiry, these formative performance tasks provide opportunities to develop the knowledge (e.g., an understanding of the book and its historical context) and practice the skills (e.g., reading sources and supporting claims with evidence) necessary to construct a coherent, evidence-based argument. The formative tasks sequence in the following way:

1. Write a summary of the plot of *Uncle Tom's Cabin* that includes main ideas and supporting details from Stowe's description of slavery in the book.

2. List four quotes in the sources that point to Stowe's motivation and write a paragraph explaining her motivation.

3. Make a T-chart comparing viewpoints expressed in newspaper reviews of *Uncle Tom's Cabin* and make a claim about the differences.

4. Participate in a structured discussion regarding the impact *Uncle Tom's Cabin* had on abolitionism.

Far more than busy work, formative performance tasks are designed as exercises to support student growth and success when approaching the summative task.

Building on the purpose and structure of the summative and formative performance tasks, extension exercises highlight the alternative ways in which students may express their arguments. For example, in the *Uncle Tom's Cabin* Inquiry, students have the opportunity to adapt their arguments into a digital documentary.

In the other inquiries, adaptations range from writing letters to the editor, engaging in a classroom debate, and participating in perspective-taking exercises.

Taking informed action experiences are designed so that students can civically engage with the content of an inquiry. Informed action can take numerous forms (e.g., discussions, debates, presentations) and can occur in a variety of contexts both inside and outside of the classroom. The key to any action, however, is the idea that it is informed. The IDM, therefore, stages the taking informed action activities such that students build their knowledge and understanding of an issue before engaging in any social action. In the *understand* stage, students demonstrate that they can think about the issues behind the inquiry in a new setting or context. The *assess* stage asks students to consider alternative perspectives, scenarios, or options as they begin to define a possible set of actions. And the *act* stage is where students decide if and how they will put into effect the results of their planning.

In the Uncle Tom's Cabin inquiry, taking informed action is expressed as three steps at the conclusion of the inquiry:

- **UNDERSTANDING:** Identify and describe a modern issue that needs reform (e.g., child labor, trafficking, poverty).

- **ASSESSING:** Create a list of possible actions that involve words, such as letters, editorials, social media, videos, and protests.

- **ACTING:** Choose one of the options and implement it as an individual, small group, or class project.

Taking informed action is included within all structured inquiries, but we acknowledge that teachers may not be able to enact the sequence due to time constraints. As we describe in the next chapter, there are ways of mitigating the time crunch—by embedding the taking informed action sequence into the formative and summative performance tasks.

Sources

With compelling and supporting questions and a series of formative and summative performance tasks in place, sources complete the IDM model. Sources provide the substance and the content for an inquiry.

In the process of constructing an inquiry, teachers can use sources in three ways:

- To spark and sustain student curiosity in an inquiry;

- To build students' disciplinary (content and conceptual) knowledge and skills;

- To enable students to construct arguments with evidence.

These three uses of sources correspond with component parts of the IDM blueprint: staging the compelling question, formative performance tasks, summative performance tasks, and additional tasks (i.e., extensions and taking informed action exercises).

Sparking curiosity is about engaging students as they initiate and sustain an inquiry. Just how to generate curiosity is, in large part, a pedagogical issue. The IDM suggests that sources can play an important role in helping students become curious about and interested in knowing more about an inquiry topic.

Each of the inquiries offers a 15-20 minute exercise, called Staging the Compelling Question, whose activities spark student curiosity. In the *Uncle Tom's Cabin* inquiry, students are asked to react to a quote by Nathaniel Hawthorne in 1848:[7]

> Words—so innocent and powerless as they are, as standing in a dictionary, how potent for good and evil they become in the hands of one who knows how to combine them.

After reading the quote, students discuss the following prompts: Does what you say matter? Does how you say something matter? How responsible should we be for the words we say and write? Next, teachers might ask students about a time when they spoke up about something they thought was unfair. This task should appeal to students' sense of fairness and introduce the idea that words can also create positive change. Using the ideas generated from the class discussion on the Hawthorne source, teachers can begin to stage the compelling question about the relationship between words and war and set the historical stage for the inquiry.

Throughout an inquiry, students encounter sources to build their disciplinary knowledge (i.e., content and concepts) and skills (e.g., historical thinking, geographic reasoning). The IDM encourages shifting instructional practice to integrate disciplinary knowledge and disciplinary skills purposefully.[8] Structured inquiries put this idea into practice through the formative and summative performance tasks.

The image below is a source for the first formative performance task in the inquiry on *Uncle Tom's Cabin*. (See Figure 3.3.) As such, it provides a powerful visual representation of an important episode in the book and key content in the inquiry. In this illustration, Eliza comes to tell Uncle Tom and his wife, Chloe, that Tom and Eliza's son, Harry, have been sold to a slave trader. Eliza had just overheard the news from her master, Mr. Shelby, that the trader will arrive in the morning to take Tom and Harry away. In a panic, Eliza plans that night to run away. The illustration and other sources in the task (another illustration and four text passages) collectively give students an opportunity to build their understanding about how Harriet Beecher Stowe described slavery through the fictionalized experiences of the characters in the book.

FIGURE 3.3: ILLUSTRATION FROM *UNCLE TOM'S CABIN*

The summative performance task in the IDM calls on students to construct and support arguments, and sources play a big role in that process. Throughout an inquiry, students examine sources through the sequence of formative performance tasks. Doing so allows students to develop the knowledge they need in order to build arguments through evidence-based claims.

Each of the sources in this inquiry holds the potential to contribute to the arguments that students might make. For example, the source on sales of *Uncle Tom's Cabin* is useful as evidence in establishing the popularity of the book. (See Table 3.2.) Using this source, students might make an inference that the popularity of this book reflected a larger abolitionist sentiment in the country. This information, combined with other information from sources, can be used as evidence to make claims about the impact of the book.

TABLE 3.2: SALES OF *UNCLE TOM'S CABIN*

DATE	SALES
June 5, 1851 – April 1, 1852	A serial publication in the *National Era* magazine has a circulation of about 8,000
March 20, 1852 – April 1, 1852	The first printing of 5,000 copies of *Uncle Tom's Cabin* sells out in two weeks.
April 2, 1852 – April 15, 1852	The second printing of 5,000 copies of *Uncle Tom's Cabin* also sells out in two weeks.
May 1852	Sales of the first edition reach 50,000
September 1852	Sales of the first edition reach 75,000
October 1852	Sales of the first edition reach 100,000
Holiday season, 1852	3,000 copies of a special illustrated edition are sold
January 1853	30,000 copies are sold of a new "Edition for the Million"
February 1853	The first foreign language version is printed in German
1852	Another 100,000 copies of a special edition printed in England are sold
Early 1853	Sales of various editions reach 310,000
End of 1853	Sales reach 1 million worldwide

It is rare that a source, as created, will be perfectly suited for use in an inquiry. Instead, most of the sources in the inquiries serve as interpretative materials, and changes to the sources are often necessary. Some sources, such as photographs, may be used as they are in an inquiry, but many sources require adaptation in one of three ways:

- **EXCERPTING.** This action involves using a portion of the source for the inquiry. Care should be taken to preserve information in the source that students may need to know about the creator and context of the source.

- **MODIFYING.** This action involves inserting definitions and/or changing the language of a text. Modifying texts increases the accessibility of sources.

- **ANNOTATING.** This action involves adding short descriptions or explanations. Annotations allow teachers to set the background context for sources.

Examples of each of these three approaches to adapting sources are evident in the middle-school inquiry on *Uncle Tom's Cabin*:

- **EXCERPTING:** Text passages from *Uncle Tom's Cabin* are all carefully selected passages from a larger text.

- **MODIFYING:** The summary of *Uncle Tom's Cabin* was slightly modified to add information about the story that was missing from the original source.

- **ANNOTATING:** The illustrations include annotations.

Some observers may object to making changes to sources, arguing that changing sources does more harm than good. When considering this point, teachers should keep in mind the purpose of the source in the inquiry and ask themselves whether they are using the source for the source's sake or to accomplish some other learning goal. It is probably rare that sources would need to be used just for the sake of using the original source.

Bringing It All Together

The IDM takes inquiry as its general starting point. A compelling question serves to initiate an inquiry; a summative performance task, where students address that question, serves to pull the inquiry together. The beginning and end points are important, but no more so than the elements—supporting questions, formative performance tasks, and sources—that comprise the middle of the Inquiry Design Model.

Using inquiry as the descriptor for the curriculum topics portrayed, however, reflects a specific, conscious decision not to produce fully-developed and comprehensive curriculum units or modules. Teachers should find considerable guidance within each inquiry around the key components of instructional design—questions, tasks, and sources. What they will not find is a complete set of prescriptive lesson plans. Experience suggests that teachers teach best the material that they mold around their particular students' needs and the contexts in which they teach. Rather than scripts reflecting generic teaching and learning situations, the IDM encourages teachers to draw on their own wealth of teaching experience as they add exercises, lessons, sources, and tasks that transform the inquiries into their own, individual pedagogical plans.

Design Considerations for a Structured Blueprint

When we build guided inquiries, we follow the 10-step IDM design process articulated in our last book, *Inquiry Design Model: Building Inquiries for the Social Studies Classroom*.[9] In that book, we outline the important design considerations for structured blueprints as designers move through the 10 steps. Not surprisingly, we think any IDM designer should read that book as a primer on inquiry design and the unique processes we follow when crafting a blueprint.

In this section, we turn our attention to alignment. Just as a builder needs to understand the entirety of a blueprint—from side to side and from top to bottom—so, too, do inquiry writers need to see how the IDM blueprint elements work as one. Builders need to take this wider view because, in the end, all the sections of a building need to be plumb, square, and fit together. To illustrate this point, we use a high school-level inquiry on the French Revolution with the compelling question, Was the French Revolution successful?

ALIGNMENT IS KEY TO A STRONG BLUEPRINT DESIGN. An IDM blueprint consists of a single page, yet there are a lot of moving elements on that page. Each element needs to make sense in and of itself, but an inquiry works only if those elements also work well together. We won't describe every possible relationship in a blueprint, but the example of a French Revolution inquiry allows us to illustrate three kinds of alignment. (See Figure 3.4 on the next page.)

FIGURE 3.4: FRENCH REVOLUTION INQUIRY

WAS THE FRENCH REVOLUTION SUCCESSFUL?

New York State Social Studies Framework Key Ideas & Practices	**10.2: ENLIGHTENMENT, REVOLUTION, AND NATIONALISM:** The Enlightenment called into question traditional beliefs and inspired widespread political, economic, and social change. This intellectual movement was used to challenge political authorities in Europe and colonial rule in the Americas. These ideals inspired political and social movements. ☑ **Gathering, Using, and Interpreting Evidence** ☑ **Chronological Reasoning and Causation** ☑ **Comparison and Contextualization**
Staging the Compelling Question	Discuss the concept of *revolution* through a series of photographs that depict the recent Egyptian uprising (2011–2013).

Supporting Question 1	Supporting Question 2	Supporting Question 3	Supporting Question 4
What were the social, economic, and political problems in prerevolutionary France?	How did the relationship between the French people and the king change in the early stages of the Revolution?	How did Robespierre justify the Reign of Terror?	Did Napoleon's rise to power represent a continuation of or an end to revolutionary ideals?
Formative Performance Task	**Formative Performance Task**	**Formative Performance Task**	**Formative Performance Task**
List social, economic, and political problems in prerevolutionary France.	Write one or two paragraphs explaining how the relationship between the French people and the king changed between 1789 and 1793.	Write a summary of Robespierre's justification for the Reign of Terror and identify two key details that support his justification.	Develop a claim supported by evidence about whether Napoleon's rise to power represents a continuation of or an end to revolutionary ideals.
Featured Sources	**Featured Sources**	**Featured Sources**	**Featured Sources**
Source A: Political cartoon of the Three Estates **Source B:** Graph of the Three Estates **Source C:** *Cahiers de Doléances* of 1789	**Source A:** Declaration of the Rights of Man and Citizen **Source B:** Declaration of the Rights of Woman and Citizen **Source C:** Decree Abolishing the Feudal System	**Source A:** Engraving of Robespierre and the guillotine **Source B:** Speech by Maximilien Robespierre	**Source A:** Napoleon's account of his coup d'état **Source B:** Painting of the *Consecration of the Emperor Napoleon I and Coronation of the Empress Josephine* **Source C:** Napoleon's account of the internal situation of France in 1804

Summative Performance Task	**ARGUMENT** Was the French Revolution successful? Construct an argument (e.g., detailed outline, poster, or essay) that addresses the compelling question, using specific claims and relevant evidence from historical sources while acknowledging competing views.
	EXTENSION Express these arguments in a perspective-taking exercise using the medium of Twitter.
Taking Informed Action	**UNDERSTAND** Investigate a current "unfinished revolution" focusing on a group of people who are currently trying to revolutionize some aspect of society. This could be a political revolution or an economic, social, or even technological revolution.
	ASSESS Examine the extent to which the current attempt at revolution is successful and state your personal stance on the justification for the revolution or whether it is, in fact, a revolution.
	ACT Write an editorial for the school or local newspaper on a current "unfinished revolution." (Within the editorial, students could discuss their positions on the efforts of those engaged in revolutionary activity and the extent to which those efforts are currently successful.)

1. COMPELLING QUESTIONS, SUMMATIVE ARGUMENT, AND ARGUMENT STEMS. In this first instance of vertical alignment, we look to the framing elements of an inquiry. The compelling question and the argument that addresses it technically define the beginning and end of an inquiry. The blueprint elements that lie in between these two poles are important. But if the question and the argument are not tightly aligned, the inquiry can quickly fall apart.

The way to keep the compelling question and summative argument in sync is through the development of argument stems. Argument stems are the responses teachers imagine their particular students might construct to answer the compelling question. Those responses need to address the question directly and suggest the kind of evidence on which students will draw.

In the first graphic below, we represent the general relationship among question, argument, and stems; the second illustrates that relationship using the example of the French Revolution. (See Figure 3.5.)

FIGURE 3.5: VERTICAL ALIGNMENT I AND THE EXAMPLE OF A FRENCH REVOLUTION INQUIRY

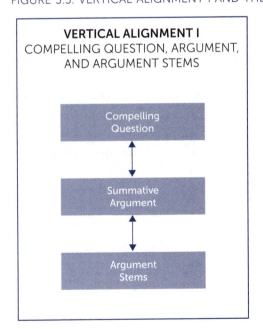

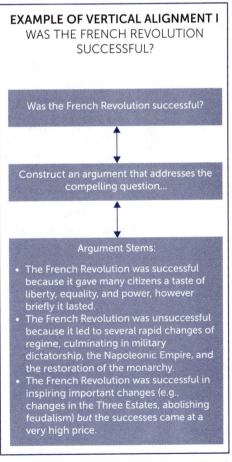

The compelling question for this inquiry—"Was the French Revolution Successful?"—offers students an opportunity to evaluate one of the signature events in European history. Rather than simply expect students to memorize a list of historical actors, events, and timelines, the question asks students to *use* this information to make and support an argument about the outcome of a French version of a national revolution.

The compelling question meets the twin tests of academic rigor and student relevance—a good start! But in order for an inquiry to be successful, the question needs to be sufficiently open ended that students can generate a range of valid, evidence-based arguments. Creating argument stems helps us pressure test these qualities of the compelling question.

The teachers who created this inquiry could imagine their students constructing a kind of "yes" response (the Revolution succeeded because it offered a vision of liberty, equality, and power), a "no" response (the Revolution was unsuccessful because it created political instability and ended in the restoration of a monarchy), and a "yes, but" response (the Revolution inspired important changes, but those changes bore a high cost).

Teachers of advanced students might imagine more ambitious stems than these, while teachers of academically challenged students might envision responses that have fewer details or are expressed in simpler terms. The key is to see within a compelling question the opportunity for students to make and support a range of substantive arguments in response to a topic or issue worth discussion. Looking at the blueprint elements vertically, then, offers inquiry writers a chance to align key relationships at the beginning of their work.

2. SUPPORTING QUESTION, FORMATIVE PERFORMANCE TASK, AND FEATURED SOURCES. Just as there needs to be convergence among the compelling question, summative argument, and argument stems, there should be congruence from a supporting question through the formative performance task to the featured sources. The formative performance task is designed to measure students' understanding of the supporting question through the use of information from the featured sources. (See Figure 3.6.)

When there is vertical task alignment, we see that the formative performance task provides an opportunity for teachers to gauge whether students understand the supporting question and have used the sources to develop knowledge and to practice the skills needed to make an argument.

Returning to the French Revolution inquiry, students begin their exploration of the compelling question with the first supporting question, "What were the social, economic, and political problems in prerevolutionary France?" In order to answer this supporting question, students explore three disciplinary sources (a political cartoon of the Three Estates, a graph depicting wealth inequality of the Three Estates, and a list of grievances of each estate) in order to complete the task of listing the social, economic, and political problems in prerevolutionary France. (See Figure 3.7.)

VERTICAL ALIGNMENT II
FORMATIVE WORK

Supporting Question

↕

Formative Performance Task

↕

Information from the Featured Sources

In this example, we simply rewrote the supporting question in order to create a formative performance task. That's not cheating by the way—it's just smart—and we use that strategy often! Teachers are often worried they haven't done enough creative work around the performance tasks. But, this is simply not the role of the formative performance task. The formative performance task has two purposes: (1) to surface students' knowledge of the supporting question, and (2) to support students in constructing their arguments. We see both things happening in this example. First, the task allows students to demonstrate whether or not they know the social, economic, and political problems in prerevolutionary France by making a list of those problems. Second, the task requires students to practice with argumentation skills by locating information from the three featured sources when making their lists of prerevolutionary problems.

FIGURE 3.7: EXAMPLE OF VERTICAL ALIGNMENT II IN A FRENCH REVOLUTION INQUIRY

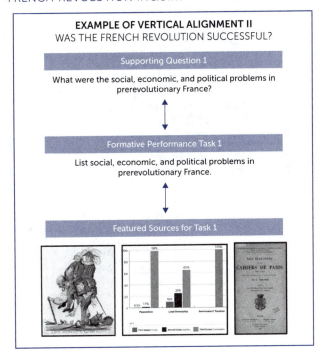

EXAMPLE OF VERTICAL ALIGNMENT II
WAS THE FRENCH REVOLUTION SUCCESSFUL?

Supporting Question 1

What were the social, economic, and political problems in prerevolutionary France?

↕

Formative Performance Task 1

List social, economic, and political problems in prerevolutionary France.

↕

Featured Sources for Task 1

3. CONCEPTUAL CLARITY FROM COMPELLING QUESTION TO TAKING INFORMED ACTION. One last kind of vertical alignment can be seen during the Finishing phase of inquiry construction. Here, the point is to check the conceptual clarity of the inquiry.

By conceptual clarity, we mean the alignment of the concept or theme around which the inquiry is built. As Figure 3.8 illustrates, conceptual clarity needs to surface in several places across a blueprint. Other concepts might hold some importance in an inquiry, but the glue that binds an inquiry together is the primary concept or theme on which students can focus.

Pulling once more on the French Revolution inquiry, we can see how the teacher-developers threaded the concept of revolution through the compelling question, the staging and formative work, and then on into the argument, extension, and taking informed action sequence.

FIGURE 3.8: VERTICAL ALIGNMENT III AND THE EXAMPLE OF A FRENCH REVOLUTION INQUIRY

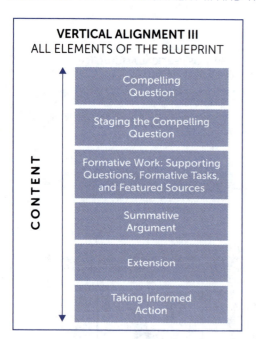

VERTICAL ALIGNMENT III
ALL ELEMENTS OF THE BLUEPRINT

CONTENT

- Compelling Question
- Staging the Compelling Question
- Formative Work: Supporting Questions, Formative Tasks, and Featured Sources
- Summative Argument
- Extension
- Taking Informed Action

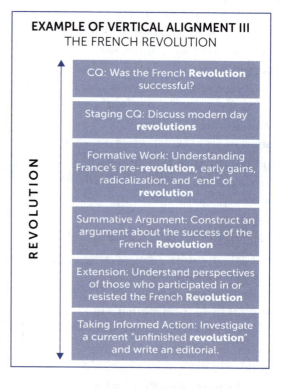

EXAMPLE OF VERTICAL ALIGNMENT III
THE FRENCH REVOLUTION

REVOLUTION

- CQ: Was the French **Revolution** successful?
- Staging CQ: Discuss modern day **revolutions**
- Formative Work: Understanding France's pre-**revolution**, early gains, radicalization, and "end" of **revolution**
- Summative Argument: Construct an argument about the success of the French **Revolution**
- Extension: Understand perspectives of those who participated in or resisted the French **Revolution**
- Taking Informed Action: Investigate a current "unfinished **revolution**" and write an editorial.

By attending to the vertical alignment of the entire inquiry, teacher-developers can clearly see any occasions in which they have lost conceptual focus. Inquiry-based practice is great fun in the teaching moment. Seeing students talking about ideas, citing sources, debating the quality of evidence—it's a social studies teacher's dream. Like every other dream realized, however, planning—lots of planning—is essential. The coherence that good inquiries display comes through the horizontal alignment evident in the question, source, and task logics described earlier. That coherence becomes even richer when the vertical dimensions of an inquiry align.

In the following section, we examine the strengths and weaknesses of teaching with structured inquiry.

Affordances and Constraints of a Structured Inquiry

Inquiry is the toughest curricular thing we do as teachers. Planning an inquiry takes time and instructing with inquiry requires additional effort. With that said, inquiry-based teaching is tremendously rewarding. One of our favorite stories about inquiry comes from an elementary classroom where students asked when recess ended while doing an IDM inquiry. The thought of social studies inquiry as an equivalent to recess just makes us smile. Because this mistake is not made often by students, we think it wise to spend this section accounting for a structured inquiry's instructional affordances and constraints. (See Table 3.2)

TABLE 3.2: INSTRUCTIONAL AFFORDANCES AND CONSTRAINTS OF A STRUCTURED INQUIRY

STRUCTURED INQUIRY	
Instructional Affordances	Instructional Constraints
Encourages students to remember their inquiry experiences.	Takes additional instructional time and energy to construct and teach with inquiry.
Makes social studies relevant to students.	May require shifts in instruction to include questioning, source work, and argumentation.
Builds students' capacity for the core academic and civic outcomes of a strong social studies education.	Enacting the Taking Informed Action sequence can become more than teachers expected.
Illustrates the value of social studies for administrators and parents.	May expose gaps in students learning which require additional skill work.

Conclusion

We use the blueprint metaphor intentionally. The blueprint serves as a plan for inquiry-based social studies instruction. Just as the blueprint for a house sketches out a plan for the rooms, walls, and dimensions of a dwelling, a curricular blueprint drafts out an inquiry experience according to its unique questions, tasks, and sources. But blueprints are tentative until they become enacted. As teachers have implemented the structured blueprints, they have pushed our thinking to adapt the blueprints for specific instructional needs. In the next chapter, we unpack the embedded action blueprint that aims to do just that.

NOTES

1. K. Swan, J. Lee, and S.G. Grant, *Inquiry Design Model: Building Inquiries in Social Studies* (Silver Spring, MD: National Council for the Social Studies and C3 Teachers, 2018).

2. R. Tyler, *Basic Principles of Curriculum and Instruction* (Chicago: University of Chicago Press, 1949); G. Wiggins and J. McTighe, *Understanding by Design* (Alexandria, VA: Association for Supervision and Curriculum Development, 1998).

3. S.G. Grant, K. Swan and J. Lee, *Inquiry-Based Practice in Social Studies Education: The Inquiry Design Model* (New York: Routledge and C3 Teachers, 2017).

4. S.G. Grant, K. Swan and J. Lee, *Inquiry-Based Practice in Social Studies Education: The Inquiry Design Model*; K. Swan, J. Lee and S.G. Grant, *Inquiry Design Model: Building Inquiries in Social Studies*.

5. This part of the chapter was written by adapting the following published work: K. Swan, J. Lee, and S. G. Grant, "The New York State Toolkit and the Inquiry Design Model: Anatomy of an Inquiry," *Social Education* 79, no. 6 (2015), 316-322.

6. J. Bruner, *The Process of Education* (Cambridge: Harvard University Press, 1960), 33.

7. N. Hawthorne, "American Note-books of Nathaniel Hawthorne," *The Atlantic Monthly* 18, no. 110 (1848). Public Domain. **https:// en.m.wikisource.org/wiki/The_Atlantic_Monthly/Volume_18/Number_110/ Passages_from_Hawthorne%27s_Note-Books**

8. K. Swan, J. Lee, and S. G. Grant, *C3 Instructional Shifts*. C3teachers.org, 2014. Retrieved from: **http://www.c3teachers.org/c3shifts/**

9. K. Swan, J. Lee and S.G. Grant, *Inquiry Design Model: Building Inquiries in Social Studies, op.cit.*

CHAPTER 4

Embedded Action Inquiry: Asking Problem-Based Compelling Questions

When we assembled a focus group of teachers at the early stages of developing the Inquiry Design Model (IDM), they wondered why action always took place at the end of an inquiry. These teachers were concerned about the time it would take to complete all the stages of an entire blueprint. Additionally, they did not want to "bury the lead." If taking informed action was so essential to being a citizen, they wanted to make it the front and center of the blueprint, particularly in problem-based inquiries where students were asked to consider solutions to a contemporary issue (e.g., What should be done about the gender wage gap?). They suggested pairing up the formative work and summative performance tasks with the understand-assess-act sequence of taking informed action so that it would save instructional time and offer a more natural approach to the civic outcome of an academic inquiry. We agreed completely and we have tried to embed action into a blueprint any time we can.

Embedding the component of taking informed action was our first major variation of the structured blueprint. To date, we have constructed two approaches to embedding action. The first approach occurs when the compelling question sets students up to solve a social problem (e.g., "Am I going to vote?") and the formative work lends itself to understanding and assessing that problem. In a second approach, we use the blueprint to structure an open-ended action experience. For example, we recently worked with a group of middle school teachers who wanted to participate in Project Citizen as a culminating experience for their sixth graders. But they wanted the project to feel less unwieldy and to be organized around questions, tasks, and sources. We varied the blueprint to help them achieve their goals.

In this chapter, we highlight both of these approaches to embedding action. We start by examining the underpinnings of civic action within the Inquiry Design Model and then examine the unique characteristics of the embedded action approach. We walk through two embedded action blueprints before ending the chapter with the challenges and opportunities of designing and teaching inquiry through an embedded action blueprint.

Civic Action

Social studies has long been criticized for its limited attention to civic engagement.[1] Learning how a bill becomes a law and how Supreme Court cases have addressed individual and group rights are useful activities. But, if students' ideas and actions are confined to the classroom, then they miss important opportunities to see how those ideas and actions play out in other public venues. IDM continues the call of the C3 Framework[2] to civic action by hardwiring this important social studies outcome into the heart of the blueprint.[3]

Taking informed action takes shape in three stages. In the *understand* stage, students demonstrate that they can think about the issues behind the inquiry in a new setting or context. The *assess* stage asks students to consider alternative perspectives, scenarios, or options as they begin to define a possible set of actions. Assessing also involves examining student efficacy or the impact of an individual's or group's actions on a particular problem. Finally, the *act* stage is where students decide if and how they will put into effect the results of their planning.

The understand-assess-act sequence of taking informed action is articulated within each IDM blueprint regardless of blueprint type. Informed action can take numerous forms (e.g., debates, public service announcements, letters to the editor) and can occur in a variety of contexts both inside and outside of the classroom. The key to any action, however, is the idea that it is *informed*. The blueprint, therefore, stages the taking informed action exercises so that students build their knowledge and understanding of an issue before engaging in any social action.

We like to think of two dimensions when we consider action opportunities: where the action takes place and how complex the action is. First, action can take place in the classroom, within the larger school grounds, or outside the school. For example, students could share ideas about an issue with another classroom or make a short presentation during the morning or afternoon announcements. In other forms of action, students interact and work with others in the community. If students speak at a town or city meeting or participate in a community protest, it will likely occur outside of school.

The other dimension of action focuses on its complexity. Complexity of action is not unlike the variety in other exercises we do in the classroom—it depends on the students. For example, some students are not afraid of public speaking whereas others are petrified. In these cases, simply presenting to another class might be far more difficult for one student than for another. So, the effort it would take for a teacher to oversee a student-led rally is likely much more complex than having students work together on something like a class position statement.

Action opportunities can occur across a long continuum of possibilities that vary greatly in location and complexity. As a starting place, teachers might encourage students to think about what action they enjoy doing, as well as how they might engage with their fellow students. Using Westheimer and Kahne's democratic citizenship framework as inspiration,[4] Muetterties and Swan delineated four dispositions for action that students might demonstrate: (1) being informed; (2) being engaged; (3) being a leader; and (4) being the change.[5] They explain the types in this way:

- To BE INFORMED, students learn about an issue and communicate that learning in some way.

- To BE ENGAGED, students engage with others on an issue. This can mean having an informed conversation, as well as volunteering on behalf of an issue/problem.

- To BE A LEADER, students organize an action to address an issue/problem.

- To BE THE CHANGE, students seek transformation, meaning they take an action that will address the root cause of an issue/problem.

Once students have considered a disposition towards action, then they can select from a myriad of ways to take action within and outside of the classroom.[6] (See Figure 4.1.)

FIGURE 4.1 DIFFERENT WAYS TO TAKE INFORMED ACTION

STEP 2: WHAT ACTION CAN I TAKE?			
Be Informed (INFORM)	Be Engaged (ENGAGE)	Be a Leader (ORGANIZE)	Be the Change (TRANSFORM)
Start conversations about your issue with others Write an article Create a pamphlet/flyer Make a video Create a public service announcement Write a story/poem/song Create a podcast Draw a picture Make a poster Create a presentation Create a class position statement Take a survey on the issue Write a suggested textbook revision	Give money to a charity related to your issue Donate items Invite a guest speaker Participate in a rally Participate in a boycott Volunteer Sign a petition Attend a candidate's forum Attend a neighborhood meeting Attend/watch a speech related to your issue Comment in an online conversation	Organize a fundraiser Organize a donation drive Organize a community service Create a Facebook page on the issue Organize a flyer campaign to raise awareness Form a club Organize a petition campaign Organize a class forum with stakeholders Organize a rally Organize a boycott Conduct a survey to determine people's views on the issue Organize a voter registration drive	Start a charity to address the cause of your issue Write a resolution to address the cause of the issue for sharing with stakeholders Contact a stakeholder about addressing your issue through policy/laws Speak at a school, town, or other community meeting Present at a local civic organization
Examples Write an essay about homelessness in your community Talk to your parents about the cleanliness of a local park	**Examples** Donate food or clothing to a food/clothing drive, homeless shelter, or other related charity Clean up litter	**Examples** Organize a food donation drive for a homeless shelter Organize a cleanup project of a local park	**Examples** Start a charity to provide job and housing supports for your community's homeless Write to your local councilperson about funding for more trash receptacles in your local park

In the next few sections, we unpack action within an embedded action blueprint. But, first, we examine the unique characteristics of an embedded action blueprint.

Characteristics of an Embedded Action Inquiry

An embedded action inquiry blueprint is designed so that students can practice taking informed action as part of the academic inquiry. The compelling question in an embedded inquiry is crafted so that students are addressing a social problem. The formative work (i.e., supporting questions, formative performance tasks, and featured sources) provides an instructional space so that students are understanding and assessing the social problem. Then, the summative argument task allows students to demonstrate what they know and how they might address the problem in a contemporary fashion. And, finally, the blueprint includes an opportunity for action that follows the argument task (See Table 4.1)

While the teacher determines most of the embedded action blueprint, it may be the case that students find sources that help them understand and assess the problem. We will take a look at this approach in the second example below on page 72 (Project Citizen: How Can I Make a Change?).

TABLE 4.1 ELEMENTS OF AN EMBEDDED ACTION INQUIRY

EMBEDDED ACTION INQUIRY	
Description	The teacher develops the inquiry, but focuses on structuring the Taking Informed Action (understand–assess–act) sequence into the core of the blueprint.
Role of Teacher and/or Student in Blueprint Development	Teacher developed
Questions	The teacher develops both the compelling and supporting questions. The compelling question typically is created so that it explores a social problem.
Tasks	The teacher develops the summative and formative tasks, but some of the formative tasks might be structured so that students are researching a supporting question.
Sources	The teacher selects most of the sources, but students might select some sources as they relate to the research opportunity.
Instructional Time	5-10 days

In the next two sections we present two examples of embedded action. In the first, we walk through an elementary-level embedded action inquiry on food insecurity and highlight its key elements of questions, tasks, and sources. In the inquiry on food insecurity, students explore food deserts, the extent to which their community is food secure, and how to advocate for a food oasis. Here, we highlight the compelling and supporting questions that frame and organize the inquiry, the assessment tasks that provide opportunities for students to demonstrate and apply their understanding, and the disciplinary sources that allow students to practice disciplinary thinking and reasoning. In the second example of an embedded inquiry, we use a blueprint that examines how students can make change through Project Citizen.

Anatomy of an Embedded Action Inquiry
Example I: Does My Community Have Enough Food?

The embedded action inquiry blueprint is similar to the structured blueprint in that it is a one-page visual representation of the questions, tasks, and sources that define an inquiry. There are compelling and supporting questions, formative and summative performance tasks, and selected disciplinary sources that help students in answering the inquiry's questions. The major difference is that the understand-assess-act sequence does not come at the end of the blueprint, but instead is embedded into the core of it.

For example, in an elementary-level food insecurity inquiry from teachers in Syracuse, New York, understanding the problem is embedded into formative performance tasks 1 and 2; assessing the problem is embedded into formative performance task 3. Acting on the problem serves as the summative extension of the argument. In this way, students have an opportunity to practice taking informed action within an inquiry rather than at the end. (See Figure 4.2) In the sections that follow, we walk through these elements in detail.

Questions

The compelling question for an embedded action inquiry asks students to address a social problem. In the food insecurity inquiry (Figure 4.2), students examine the question, "Does my community have enough food?"

What makes this question compelling? First, we think it is academically rigorous. In order to understand the question, students need to understand what makes an urban food desert, the detrimental impacts that surface when there is a lack of access to healthy food, and how communities have worked to remedy the problem. In building these understandings, students need to think through multiple disciplinary lenses including geography, economics, and civic thinking in order to understand the extent of the problem.

We also think the question is student-friendly. Humans can all relate to food because we need it to survive. Young students in particular may organize their school days around food, which includes lunch time. In schools where there is a high percentage of free and reduced lunch, students are particularly in tune to food insecurity. This inquiry was developed for a student population in which access to healthy food is a real problem and where food insecurity is a major issue for families. The inquiry allows students to examine and

FIGURE 4.2: AN EMBEDDED ACTION INQUIRY BLUEPRINT ON FOOD INSECURITY

DOES MY COMMUNITY HAVE ENOUGH FOOD?	
Syracuse City Curriculum Key Idea	**3.9** Communities meet their need and wants in a variety of ways forming the basis for their economy **3.10** Each community develops an economic system that answers: What will be produced? How will it be produced? For whom will it be produced?
Staging the Compelling Question	Where do we buy food? Brainstorm the different places where you buy food.

Supporting Question 1	Supporting Question 2	Supporting Question 3
Understand	*Understand*	*Assess*
What is a food desert?	Is my school in a food desert?	Where does my community need food the most?
Formative Performance Task	**Formative Performance Task**	**Formative Performance Task**
Create an infographic illustrating features of a food desert.	Write a description of the school's level of food insecurity.	Write a claim or series of claims about where more food options are needed.
Featured Sources	**Featured Sources**	**Featured Sources**
Source A: American Nutrition Association definition **Source B:** United States Department of Agriculture (USDA) definition **Source C:** "Poor people cannot find fresh and healthy food," 2014	**Source A:** Mapping the Food Environment in Syracuse, New York, 2017	*See previous featured sources*

Summative Performance Task	**ARGUMENT** Does my community have enough food? Construct an argument (e.g., graphic) about whether your community has enough food using at least one claim and evidence from the inquiry.	
Taking Informed Action	**ACT OPTIONS: City "Food Oasis"** **ACT** Contact the Onondaga County Health Department or your city council member with suggestions for your area to help people have easier access to healthy food (e.g., add more food options, expand bus routes, community gardens, etc.)	**ACT OPTIONS: School-level "Food Oasis"** **ACT** Write a proposal to the principal to build a community garden at the school **ACT** Write a proposal to the principal to have a food bank at the school; conduct a food drive **ACT** Write a proposal to the school board about having food banks in schools in food deserts

address an issue that is close to their community and to be part of a solution.

The supporting questions help to break the compelling question into manageable chunks of content. They also sequence the key ideas in such a way that students can understand the problem of food insecurity and assess what role they might play in addressing the problem. For example, the first two supporting questions ask students to define a food desert (Supporting Question 1: "What is a food desert?") and determine whether their school is in a food desert (Supporting Question 2: "Is my school in a food desert?"). The third supporting question provides an instructional space for students to assess where their community might need food the most (Supporting Question 3: "Where does my community need food the most?").

Taken together, the compelling and supporting questions provide a content path for the inquiry. In this way, we suggest that there is a question logic that holds the inquiry together. In other words, the supporting questions, formative performance tasks, and featured sources sequence in a coherent way across the blueprint. These sequences build progressively upon one another, becoming the instructional path of the inquiry. That path must be clear and connected to the framing elements of the inquiry—not circuitous or meandering. In other words, we want the lines between the compelling question and the summative argument task to be as straight as possible.

In the food insecurity inquiry above, the supporting questions are sequenced so that this logic or coherence becomes apparent around the understand-assess progression.

Tasks

Similar to the structured blueprint, the formative tasks in an embedded inquiry allow students to check their understandings of the supporting questions. In the food insecurity inquiry, students answer the supporting questions by tackling three formative performance tasks that move them to a summative argument task. The formative tasks sequence in the following way:

1. Create an infographic illustrating features of a food desert.

2. Write a description of the school's level of food insecurity.

3. Write a claim or series of claims about where more food options are needed.

When crafting inquiries, we like to see a task logic emerge across the formative performance tasks. In this inquiry, the task logic is constructed so that students are acquiring important content knowledge at the same time that they are practicing argumentation skills.

Elementary students might struggle a bit with language and fluency as they are emergent readers and writers at that age. In this inquiry, when we ask students to "make a claim about where their community needs food," it may be a single sentence such as the following:

CLAIM: Places around my school need food.

- EVIDENCE 1: There are only corner stores around the school.

- EVIDENCE 2: There are no grocery stores close by the school.

- EVIDENCE 3: Many people in my community do not have a car to drive to a store.

These types of claim-making exercises can be done individually or collaboratively in groups and with or without the assistance of a teacher. Collectively, the formative performance tasks lead students to construct an evidence-based argument in response to the compelling question, "Does my community need food?" Students' arguments will likely vary, but could include any of the following argument stems as a starting place:

- My community has enough food because it is near many different places where we can buy healthy things to eat.

- My community is in a food desert because it does not have many places where we can buy healthy things to eat.

- Though my school/my home is close to places with healthy foods, many other places in my community do not have enough healthy foods.

Now that students have examined key questions that help them understand and assess an issue and have demonstrated their understandings through the summative argument, they are ready to act. In this way, the summative argument task serves as the foundation for the action. For the food insecurity inquiry, students might act by contacting the local county health department or a city council member with suggestions for the district to help people have easier access to healthy food. Suggestions could take many forms: locations of food stores with healthier and affordable food options, suggestions for bus routes to help increase access to food stores, the establishment of community gardens, or advocacy for a school-based food oasis.

It is important to note that this is a suggested action for this particular school district. It may be the case that in the course of the inquiry students want to act by doing something else. We always encourage student agency when it comes to action, and support amending inquiries to best meet students' needs.

Sources

Students encounter five sources within this inquiry that help them build up their understandings around food insecurity and food deserts. The first source is an image bank of food spaces including a grocery store, gas station, farmers market, and fast food restaurant. (See Figure 4.3.) Students encounter these sources when they work through the Staging the Compelling Question exercise which asks them to brainstorm places where people buy food.

FIGURE 4.3: IMAGE BANK OF FOOD SOURCES FOR FOOD INSECURITY INQUIRY

Image 1: Grocery store / Supermarket | Pixabay, Open License

Image 2: Gas Station / Corner store | Flickr, CC BY-SA 2.0

Image 3: Farmer's Market: CNY Regional Market in Syracuse | Wikimedia Commons, CC BY-SA 4.0

Image 4: McDonalds in Syracuse, NY | Screenshot from Google Maps

Supporting question 1 includes three text-based sources that help to define a food desert. Featured Source A is a definition of a food desert authored by the American Nutrition Association. Included within the definition is the traveling distance to a place where people can access healthy food. In urban areas, convenient traveling distance is one mile; in rural areas, convenient traveling distance is 10 miles. Students should be encouraged to map their own area and discuss why the recommended distance is shorter for urban than for rural areas.

Featured Source B builds on students' emergent understandings by providing the United States Department of Agriculture definition of food deserts and the factors that impact access to healthy foods. We adapted the text so that it would be more accessible for all student reading levels:

> The Farm Bill (2008) defines a food desert as places in the United States that have less access to affordable and healthy foods. Many different things impact access to healthy foods.
>
> In terms of travel, access will be impacted by whether or not the person owns a car or has a disability, which may limit how they travel to places. Other factors in a community impact access, such as how many sidewalks there are and whether there are enough bus stops for people to get to a food store with healthy options.
>
> How much food costs impacts access, as well. If healthy food is too expensive, not all people will be able to afford healthy, nutritious options.

And, finally, Featured Source C is an article published in the *Philadelphia Inquirer* in 2014 that was adapted for young readers by *Newsela*. Entitled "Poor People Cannot Find Fresh and Healthy Food," the article lays out the problem of healthy versus unhealthy food. Together, these three featured sources help students in creating an infographic illustrating features of a food desert.

For supporting question 2, students mine a report by the local government that contains information about food deserts in Syracuse, New York. Students use their zip code to explore and analyze data about their particular area. For each zip code, the report includes the following information: population total, ethnic composition, age percentages, median household income, percent living in poverty (overall and children), households without a vehicle, households using Supplemental Nutrition Assistance Program benefits, population living with a disability, percentage born outside of the United States, and percentage of adults without a high school degree. (See Figure 4.4.)

FIGURE 4.4. SCREEN SHOTS OF DATA FROM THE ONONDAGA COUNTY HEALTH DEPARTMENT

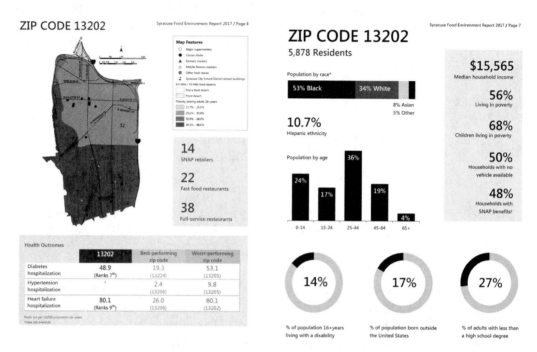

"Mapping the Food Environment in Syracuse New York 2017," Onondaga County Health Department. | Accessed from: http://www.ongov.net/health/documents/FoodEnvironment.pdf

Students can also use the data and information from the sources in supporting questions 1 and 2 to answer supporting question 3. Particularly with younger students, we prefer having fewer disciplinary sources so that they do not overwhelm the inquiry process. It is important to note that the five sources included in this inquiry could be adapted for different locales.

In the next section, we examine a different approach to embedded action. In this example, the blueprint allows for an open-ended action experience.

Anatomy of an Embedded Action Inquiry
Example 2: How Can I Make A Change?

There are many action-oriented projects in social studies. Project Citizen, Mikva Challenge, and National History Day are all programs that assist teachers in helping students become active citizens. Many teachers want to do this kind of project-based work, but find launching and sustaining it challenging. Such was the case with a group of sixth-grade teachers in Illinois.

Teachers in this district wanted to end the school year with a six-week exploration of a public policy using the curricular platform, Project Citizen. Project Citizen encourages students to work together to identify a problem that impacts their community and "then research the problem, evaluate alternative solutions, develop their own solution in the form of a public policy, and create a political action plan to enlist local or state authorities to adopt their proposed policy."[7] Students ultimately present their project in a public showcase for community members as well as policy makers. Doing so sounds a lot like the taking informed action sequence of understand, assess, and act.

While the teachers were committed to the project, they did not quite know how to structure it within the IDM inquiry model they had come to use. So, they began to play around with the blueprint and designed the following embedded action inquiry. (See Figure 4.5 on page 72.) In the sections that follow, we walk through the questions, tasks, and sources to demonstrate how these teachers aligned the project to the embedded action inquiry blueprint.

Questions

The compelling question for this inquiry is simply, "How can I make a change?" This broad-brush question allows students room for determining what matters to them and to their community. That is half of the compelling question criteria right there—it is relevant to students. As for its academic rigor, what could be more important than elevating students into thoughts of their own agency when addressing problems that face citizens? We think this could be one of the most compelling questions we have seen.

The supporting questions are staged to offer students an opportunity to understand and assess an issue. In the understand and assess stages, students grapple with two supporting questions, "What do people need to know about the issue or problem?" and "What are other ways people could address the issue or problem?" These

PROJECT CITIZEN: HOW CAN I MAKE A CHANGE?

Illinois Social Science Standards	**SS.CV.3.6-8.LC, MdC, MC:** Compare the means by which individuals and groups change societies, promote the common good, and protect rights. **SS.CV.5.6-8.LC; MdC; MC:** Apply civic virtues and democratic principles in school and community settings.
Staging the Compelling Question	What is something important to me? Students determine an issue or problem that is of interest to them.

Supporting Question 1	Supporting Question 2	Supporting Question 3	Supporting Question 4
Understand and Assess		*Plan*	
What do people need to know about the issue/problem?	What are other ways people could address the issue/problem?	What policy best addresses the issue/problem?	What can I do to address the issue/problem?
Formative Performance Task	**Formative Performance Task**	**Formative Performance Task**	**Formative Performance Task**
Task 1: Explaining the Problem	*Task 2: Examining the Alternative Policies*	*Task 3: Proposing a Public Policy*	*Task 4: Developing an Action Plan*
Create a list of things people should know about the issue/problem.	Make a T-Chart listing the pros and cons of solutions that would address the issue/problem.	Construct an evidentiary claim on the best way to address the issue/problem.	Develop a plan to address the issue/problem.
Featured Sources	Featured Sources	Featured Sources	Featured Sources
Source A: *Scholastic News* **Source B:** *Time for Kids* **Source C:** *Newsela*	*See featured sources for Supporting Question 1*	*See featured sources for Supporting Question 1*	*See featured sources for Supporting Question 1*

Summative Performance Task	**ARGUMENT** How can I make a change? Construct an argument about how they will make change, including a step-by-step plan with anticipated timeline.
	ACT Implement the taking informed civic action plan in a way that shares the project with others.
	EXTENSION Reflect on the experience noting what you learned from the project and what you might do differently next time.

foundational questions help to provide shape and direction to the project.

For this inquiry, the teachers also added an additional step to the taking informed action sequence--planning. Supporting questions 3 and 4 allow students to drill down on a particular solution (What policy best addresses the issue or problem?) and how the students might carve out a slice of the solution (What can I do to address the issue/problem?).

Together, these four supporting questions provide a path from the compelling question to the summative performance task.

Tasks

The formative performance tasks were inspired by some of the steps outlined in Project Citizen:[8]

- Task 1: Explaining the problem.

- Task 2: Examining the alternative policies.

- Task 3: Proposing a public policy.

- Task 4: Developing an action plan.

The teachers took these broad steps and created formative performance tasks building a task logic around argumentation. The formative performance tasks appear as follows:

FORMATIVE PERFORMANCE TASK 1: Create a list of things people should know about the issue/problem.

FORMATIVE PERFORMANCE TASK 2: Make a T-Chart listing the pros and cons of solutions that would address the issue/problem.

FORMATIVE PERFORMANCE TASK 3: Construct an evidentiary claim on the best way to address the issue/problem.

FORMATIVE PERFORMANCE TASK 4: Develop a plan to address the issue/problem.

Like other IDM blueprints, students work through the formative performance tasks to arrive at an evidence-based argument that answers the compelling question before moving to more expressive tasks. Students use the argument task to outline their plan and to defend it with evidence from their inquiry. Then, they are able to act by implementing their plan.

One interesting addition that the teachers made was to include an extension at the end of the inquiry. In the extension, students are asked to reflect on their project noting what they learned and what they might do differently next time. This reflection step, a major component of Project Citizen, was easily accommodated within the blueprint structure.

Sources

The featured sources for this inquiry include three news databases that assist students in understanding the issue or problem in supporting question 1. (See Table 4.2.)

TABLE 4.2: SOURCES FOR THE MAKING CHANGE INQUIRY

Source A: *Scholastic News*	This publication provides news articles for students based on age/ability level. Subscription required. Accessed from: **https://sn3.scholastic.com/**
Source B: *Time for Kids*	This publication provides news articles for students based on age/ability level. Subscription required. Accessed from: **https://www.timeforkids.com/**
Source C: *Newsela*	Newsela provides news articles from major publications, adapted to different ability levels. Requires a free account. Accessed from: **https://newsela.com/**

Teachers may want to supplement these sources once students have determined the problem they will tackle within the inquiry.

Design Considerations for an Embedded Action Inquiry

Once we started playing with embedded action in inquiries like the food insecurity and Project Citizen inquiries above, we try now to do it as often as possible. We recognize that classroom time is limited, especially for social studies, and informed action can be woven into the heart of many an inquiry for both practical and philosophical reasons. Students should walk away from a social studies class believing that the academic content and skills they learn throughout an inquiry are relevant to the world in which they live. To the extent that action can be incorporated into the formative work of an inquiry, we always choose that design route.

In the following set of design considerations, we provide additional suggestions for crafting embedded action inquiry blueprints.

PROVIDE OPTIONS FOR ACTION. As we noted above, students should have agency when practicing informed action. In many inquiries, we see teachers providing options in the taking informed action sequence so that students can feel that the action is not forced and can be reflective of the ways they feel most comfortable expressing their civic voices. Ultimately, students can choose from their list of actions and implement an action with others or individually (see Figure 4.1 on page 62). In this way, action is authentic and is owned by the students.

No citizen we know likes to be told how and when to speak up. Self-determination is a fundamental tenet of living in a democracy that emphasizes freedom of speech and the right of people to peaceably assemble and to appeal to the government. Taking informed action opportunities should reflect our rights as citizens and provide curricular spaces that encourage students to step up and be heard on issues that are raised within an inquiry.

AVOID MADE-UP PROBLEMS. With the rise in popularity of project-based learning, we have also witnessed an increase in curricular creativity. Social studies has long needed a reboot, but some creativity may go too far—particularly if students are to practice civic action. For example, one unit we have seen is around a fictitious zombie apocalypse. In this unit (and there are many variations on the web), students are asked, "How can social studies keep you alive during a zombie apocalypse?" From there, students are to use the disciplinary strands of the social studies (anthropology, economics, geography) to stave off a monster invasion. Although we could argue about the merits of this kind of activity, it is particularly challenging for an embedded action inquiry. Taking informed action is about authentic action and elevating students' understanding of civic engagement. If these exercises come off as phony or contrived, students may get the wrong message about civic outreach. For better or worse, we have enough real problems to solve in this world and embedded action inquiry is better suited for these than for zombies.

BE INNOVATIVE WITH EMBEDDING ACTION. While some creativity may be a bridge too far, we do encourage teachers to innovate with the blueprint. In fact, curricular invention is what prompted us to write this book. Teachers wanting to think outside the original boxes of the structured blueprint have helped us to create the embedded action blueprint as well as the focused, guided, and student-directed blueprints that are articulated in the next few chapters.

One such innovation around embedded action that emerged during the New York Toolkit project is a 12th grade inquiry on voting that features the compelling question, "Am I going to vote?" Teachers used the Staging the Compelling Question exercise to have students understand and assess whether they were going to vote. (See Figure 4.6 on page 76.) As students move through the inquiry, they examine trends in youth voting and voter apathy before constructing an argument that addresses the compelling question. Ultimately, students act by either registering or not registering to vote. Although it would break our social studies educator hearts for students to decide not to vote, students get to opt in to our democracy and to choose to exercise individual agency (as painful as their choices might be!).

FIGURE 4.6: AN EMBEDDED ACTION INQUIRY BLUEPRINT ON VOTING

AM I GOING TO VOTE?

New York State Social Studies Framework Key Ideas & Practices	**12.G3 RIGHTS, RESPONSIBILITIES, AND DUTIES OF CITIZENSHIP:** Active, engaged, and informed citizens are critical to the success of the United States' representative democracy. United States citizens have certain rights, responsibilities, and duties, the fulfillment of which help to maintain the healthy functioning of national, state, and local communities. ☑ **Gathering, Using, and Interpreting Evidence** ☑ **Civic Participation**
Staging the Compelling Question	**UNDERSTAND** Investigate the registration process for voting. **ASSESS** Discuss whether or not students in class would or could register to vote.

Supporting Question 1	Supporting Question 2	Supporting Question 3
How has the youth voter changed over time?	What are the reasons some youth choose to vote?	What are the reasons some youth choose not to vote?
Formative Performance Task	**Formative Performance Task**	**Formative Performance Task**
List short-term and long-term trends in the youth voting record.	Develop a claim supported by evidence that answers the supporting question.	Develop a claim supported by evidence that answers the supporting question.
Featured Sources	**Featured Sources**	**Featured Sources**
Source A: Census demographic data, 1964–2012 **Source B:** "Youth Voters Supported Obama Less, But May Have Mattered More"	**Source A:** "The Fight for the Right to Vote in the United States" **Source B:** "I Make Government Work" **Source C:** "Youth Voting Quick Facts"	**Source A:** "Why Don't Youth Vote: Young People Respond" **Source B:** "Why Young People Don't Vote" **Source C:** "Youth Vote"

Summative Performance Task	**ARGUMENT** Construct an argument (e.g., detailed outline, poster, essay) that addresses the compelling question "Am I going to vote?" using specific claims and relevant evidence from historical sources while acknowledging competing perspectives. **EXTENSION** Participate in a class discussion on their decisions to register or not register to vote by examining whether or not they are likely to vote in the next presidential election. **ACT** Register to vote or decide not to register to vote.

Affordances and Constraints of an Action Inquiry

Teachers often share with us that taking informed action is the scariest part of the blueprint. While academic inquiry is confined to the classroom, action opportunities can expand outside of it. Whether students invite a guest speaker or they organize a fundraiser, other students, educators, parents, and community members will be involved. And, doing so is understandably scary. There are just more instructional variables to account for when doing action and teaching with inquiry is already hard enough.

With that said, it is these kinds of authentic experiences that often stay with students and change others' minds about the necessity and meaning of the social studies. In the following table, we account for the instructional affordances and constraints on embedded action inquiry, and try to be honest about the real challenges and benefits of tackling what is likely the most intimidating part of the inquiry arc.

TABLE 4.3: INSTRUCTIONAL AFFORDANCES AND CONSTRAINTS ON EMBEDDED ACTION INQUIRY

ACTION INQUIRY	
Instructional Affordances	Instructional Constraints
Makes social studies relevant to students.	Takes additional instructional time and energy to coordinate.
Builds students' capacity for the core academic and civic outcomes of a strong social studies education.	Engaging in action can become more than teachers anticipate.
Helps administrators and parents see value in social studies if it is built around real problems and students taking action.	

Conclusion

Social studies teachers are both inventive and efficient. We are inspired by the many changes to the blueprint offered by teachers who have kicked its tires. Some of that innovation comes from the need to be instructionally efficient. We definitely see that need come through when we embed action into the core of the inquiry. In the next chapter, we examine another efficient curricular blueprint—the focused inquiry.

NOTES

1. D. Campbell, M. Levinson, and F. Hess (Eds.), *Making Civics Count: Citizenship Education for a New Generation* (Boston: Harvard University Press, 2012); P. Levine, *The Future of Democracy: Developing the Next Generation of American Citizens* (Lebanon, NH: University Press of New England, 2007); M. Levinson, *No Citizen Left Behind* (Boston: Harvard University Press, 2014).

2. National Council for the Social Studies (NCSS), *College, Career, and Civic Life (C3) Framework for Social Studies State Standards* (Silver Spring, MD: NCSS, 2013).

3. S.G. Grant, K. Swan and J. Lee, *Inquiry-Based Practice in Social Studies Education: The Inquiry Design Model* (New York: Routledge and C3Teachers, 2017).

4. J. Westheimer and J. Kahne, "What Kind of Citizen? The Politics of Educating for Democracy," *American Educational Research Journal* 41, no. 2 (2004), 237–269.

5. C. Muetterties and K. Swan, "Be The Change: Guiding Students to Take Informed Action," *Social Education* 83, no. 4 (September 2019), 232-237.

6. *Ibid.*

7. Center for Civic Education. *Project Citizen*. Retrieved from **http://www.civiced.org/ programs/project-citizen**

8. *Ibid.*

Focused Inquiry: Collapsing the Blueprint to Focus on a Disciplinary Skill or Concept

How many times should I do inquiry in a year? This is the number one question that educators ask us about inquiry and we understand why. One of the inescapable challenges to inquiry is its lack of efficiency in "covering" content. Inquiry typically takes longer than direct instruction and this reality can be problematic for teachers struggling to find time to cover the breadth of content outlined in many social studies courses. For example, a typical U.S. history curriculum asks teachers in one grade level to cover the settlement of North America by Native Americans up to the Civil War and then teach another course to cover the period of Reconstruction to the modern day. Most teachers need to balance content coverage with the demands of inquiry.

The first move that teachers who are feeling the pinch of time might make is to cut down on the number of sources in an inquiry. Fewer sources limit the amount of time needed for the inquiry and limit the content covered. Not enough time for inquiry? Cut the sources, reduce the content. But you know what that means: It increases the pressure to cover more content later, ugh! It's a vicious cycle indeed, and sometimes results in teachers just giving up on inquiry all together. Focused inquiries aim to disrupt this cycle by adding value to shorter inquiries with more targeted sources and an intentional focus on important skills or concepts.

We know that many teachers have their students practice particular skills within the social studies disciplines (e.g., cause and effect, deliberation) and want to do so through an inquiry-based approach. Focused inquiries provide teachers with an approach to doing just that—zoom in so that students work with narrowly focused sources and practice particular skills toward developing their expertise in source work. We also know that students are able to develop important conceptual understandings through inquiry. Focused inquiries enable teachers to concentrate on specific conceptual understandings that support students' broader content knowledge.

In this chapter, we describe the unique capacity of a focused inquiry to zero in on concepts and skills through rigorous source work. We then unpack the elements of the focused blueprint by looking at an example and its questions, tasks, and sources. Next, we turn to the design of these types of blueprints suggesting a process for development by starting with a particular source or source set that amplifies a particular skill or concept. We conclude the chapter by discussing design considerations and the affordances and constraints of this type of inquiry experience.

Focusing on Concepts, Skills, and Sources

What makes a focused inquiry, *focused*? The short answer is, fewer tasks and sources and thus less instructional time. You may ask, if that's all there is to a focused inquiry, then why all the fuss. Why an entire chapter on focused inquiry? The long answer is in how we derive the *focus* in a focused inquiry. The fundamental quality of a focused inquiry is its concentration on social studies skills *and* concepts through the examination of disciplinary sources.

One of the perennial (and frankly silly) debates in education is whether content or skills is the most important component of a social studies education. Standing alone, content (represented in sources and conceptual knowledge) is easily critiqued as boring, unimportant, or even dangerous.[1] Skills alone are an even bigger and more villainous boogeyman to some.[2] But, here is the point: practicing skills and surfacing concepts are equally important aims of inquiry-based instruction. Students cannot inquire about nothing; they have to inquire about content. The way we make any content important is by grafting it on to an important concept. And, the way we practice skills and create understanding of concepts and particular pieces of content is through the examination of sources. (See Figure 5.1)

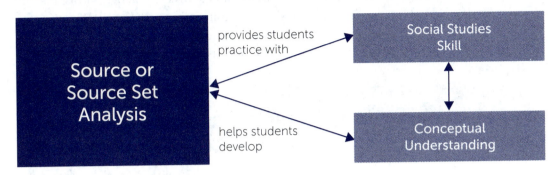

This focus on either sources and skills or concepts drives the inquiry design and implementation in the classroom in a logical way. In a focused inquiry, we utilize specific sources to assist students in practicing a particular social studies skill and/or developing a conceptual understanding.

Inquiry designers put sources, skills, and concepts into motion when creating inquiries. Just like compelling and supporting questions depend on one another, sources, skills, and concepts are also interdependent. Let's take a moment to think through this relationship by looking at two examples.

If a teacher wanted her students to practice perspective-taking (a social studies disciplinary skill), she could set up an instructional experience that animates that skill. She might choose a controversial figure like Christopher Columbus, Malcolm X, or Margaret Thatcher to enable students to see each person through multiple lenses or perspectives. But, she could not stop there. In order to have students practice the perspective-taking skill, she would need to choose disciplinary sources that articulate the range of perspectives. In this way, a skill (perspective-taking) is dependent on the concept (Colonialism) which is then dependent on the source set (two vastly different images of Christopher Columbus). (See Figure 5.2 on page 82; the images are reproduced in more detail on page 91.)

The same relationship is true if we reverse the exercise by starting with a concept. If a teacher wanted to teach a concept like inequity, he would need to think about the sources that would enable students to analyze that idea. He may use a table or graph that shows income distribution in the U.S. as a means of depicting inequalities in economic capacity. In selecting that source, the teacher is asking students to practice skills like gathering information from a source and using economic data. As you can see, the interplay between concepts and skills and sources is inextricable. The notion that students could work with disciplinary sources, practice with skills, or develop conceptual knowledge about nothing is absurd. We expect that it goes without saying that a focused inquiry must be driven by interesting social studies content. (See Figure 5.3)

FIGURE 5.2: SKILLS, CONCEPTS, AND SOURCES LINKED THROUGH A COLUMBUS EXAMPLE

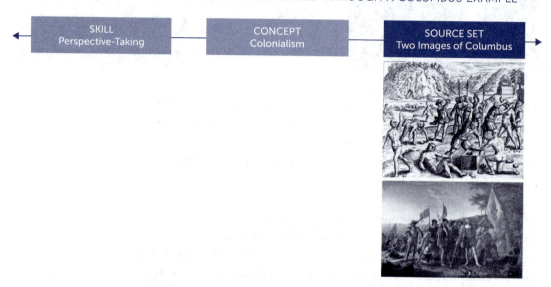

FIGURE 5.3: CONCEPTS, SOURCES, SKILLS LINKED THROUGH AN ECONOMIC INEQUITY EXAMPLE

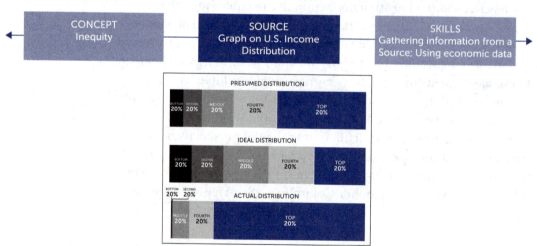

With this reminder about the importance of content in focusing an inquiry, you may need a little skill-based or conceptual inspiration for a focused inquiry. The C3 Framework is there for you.[3] The C3 Framework details disciplinary and literacy skills that are essential for success in college, career, and civic life.[4] The literacies described in the C3 Framework fall into two broad categories—those skills needed for inquiry such as questioning, evaluating evidence, and communicating conclusions and those grounded in academic concepts and approaches to organizing and making sense out of disciplinary content. The C3 inquiry literacies contained within the Framework are carefully and explicitly articulated in Dimensions 1, 3, and 4 or the Inquiry Arc, and include the following:

C3 INQUIRY LITERACIES

1. Questioning

2. Selecting sources

3. Gathering information from sources

4. Evaluating sources

5. Making claims

6. Using evidence

7. Constructing arguments and explanations

8. Adapting arguments and explanations

9. Presenting arguments and explanations

10. Critiquing arguments and explanations

11. Analyzing social problems

12. Assessing options for action

13. Taking Informed Action

The disciplinary literacies contained within Dimension 2 are more deeply embedded within the indicators. The following list provides some clarifying examples of literacies that are featured in one or more of the indicators in Dimension 2.

C3 DISCIPLINARY LITERACIES

1. Using deliberative processes

2. Participating in school settings

3. Following rules

4. Making economic decisions

5. Using economic data

6. Identifying prices in a market

7. Reasoning spatially

8. Constructing maps

9. Using geographic data

10. Classifying historical sources

11. Determining the purpose of an historical source

12. Analyzing cause and effect in history

13. Understanding how historical perspectives change

For a refresher on key concepts in social studies, you may want to examine Table 5.1 below. It is by no means an exhaustive list, but rather a starting place for focusing your inquiry on a concept.

TABLE 5.1: DISCIPLINARY CONCEPTS IN SOCIAL STUDIES

GOVERNMENT	ECONOMICS	HISTORY	GEOGRAPHY	GLOBAL CONNECTIONS
Citizenship	Scarcity	Time	Space	System
Principles—Justice	Allocation	Change	Place	Interdependence
Rule of Law	Resources	Continuity	Location	Human Rights
Law and Regulation	Needs/Wants	Era	Region	International Law
Power	Choice	Culture	Human-Environment Interaction	Global Economy
Authority	Tradeoff	Origins	Connections	Alliance
Democracy	Incentives	Civilization	Culture	Cooperation
Republic	Opportunity Cost	Exploration	Adaptation	Communication
Sovereignty	Standard of Living	Migration	Diffusion	Complexity
Nation-States	Markets	Conquest	Resources	Crisis
Institutions	Trade	Conflict	Globalization	Invasion
Rights and Responsibilities	Gains from Trade	Consequences	Climate	Genocide
Individual/Group	Exchange	Colonialism	Patterns	Terrorism
Civic Engagement	Supply and Demand	Revolution	Population	Peace
Politics	Competition	Independence	Distribution	Climate Change
Compromise	Producer/Consumer	Nationalism	Population Density	
Federalism	Productivity	Sectionalism	Scale	
Constitutionalism	Efficiency	Isolationism	Boundary/Gradient	
Checks and Balances	Distribution	Progressivism	Urban/Rural	
Domestic/Foreign Policy	Regulation	Industrialization	City/County/State	
Conflict	Taxation	Invention		
Diversity	Budget, Surplus, Deficit	Innovation		
Privacy	Inflation, Depression, Recession			
	Unemployment			
	Investment			

It is important to note that all inquiry provides an opportunity for students to build up their conceptual understandings, to practice disciplinary and inquiry-based skills, and to do so through source work. What makes focused inquiries *focused*, is a designer's laser-like attention to these elements specifically. Clarity is the key with focused inquiry. Being clear about the focus (the concept, skill, and sources) allows the inquiry designer to remove the fluff and to get to the essence of the inquiry.

In the next section, we examine a focused inquiry—How should we remember Columbus?-- that aims to have students consider how historical perspectives change over time by looking at a controversial figure from the past.

Characteristics of a Focused Inquiry

The original IDM blueprint is structured so that students explore a compelling question through supporting questions, formative and summative performance tasks, and a range of disciplinary sources.[5] The inquiry crescendoes into an evidence-based argument, which can be broadened through an expressive extension and/or a civic experience. Teachers play an important role in this process by engaging students in the compelling question, scaffolding their source work, and ensuring that they are mastering the content and developing skills through the successive formative performance tasks. Ultimately, we suggest that teaching the IDM structured blueprint will take between 3-10 days of instruction.

But teachers do not always have 3-10 days of instruction for any one topic. Moreover, many IDM-inspired teachers want more flexibility in its implementation, so that they can target particular skills and/or concepts. These teachers have mined IDM for its essence—questions, tasks, and sources—and have treated the blueprint as a pedagogical accordion expanding and contracting based on the needs of their students as well as their curricular scope and sequence. Some have expanded outward, developing longer inquiry experiences, while others have condensed their inquiries by focusing on an inquiry concept or skill.

In a focused inquiry, there is still a compelling question to be answered by an evidence-based argument, but the question is narrower in scope and the argumentative task could consist of a single claim and counterclaim. Instead of 3-4 supporting questions with the attendant formative tasks and disciplinary sources, there are only 1-2. Staging the compelling question has always been a limited exercise, so it remains as is in a focused inquiry. The end of the blueprint, which can stretch out if desired, features either an extension or an action opportunity, but not both. Overall, the focused inquiry shrinks the instructional demands to one to two class periods. (See Table 5.2 on page 86.)

TABLE 5.2: THE ELEMENTS OF A FOCUSED INQUIRY

FOCUSED INQUIRY	
Description	The teacher develops the inquiry, but focuses on a particular source or source set that assists students in practicing a disciplinary skill (e.g., classify and evaluate history as change and/or continuity), and/or a concept (e.g., human settlement).
Role of Teacher and/ or Student in Blueprint Development	Teacher-Developed
Questions	The teacher develops a compelling question to be narrower in scope and to (typically) wrap tightly around a social studies skill or concept. The teacher develops 1-2 supporting questions to explore the compelling question.
Tasks	The teacher develops summative and formative performance tasks. The summative task could consist of a single claim and/or counter-claim. The teacher develops an exercise for staging the compelling question that introduces the compelling question and either an extension or an action experience. There are 1-2 formative performance tasks that measure students' understanding of the 1-2 supporting questions.
Sources	The teacher selects fewer sources that directly "talk to one another" or even a single source that helps teachers collapse instructional time.
Instructional Time	1-2 days

It is important to note that focused inquiries are still grounded in the core elements of the original blueprint—questions, tasks, and sources. Teachers tell us that having flexibility allows them to stitch together different kinds of inquiry-based experiences, increase their frequency, and move their instructional practices so that inquiry lives in rather than simply visits their classrooms. When we asked a C3 Teacher, Ryan New, how often he does inquiry, he promoted its everyday value:

> Since IDM, I have made questions, tasks, and sources the soul of my instructional practice. I have found that if you only visit inquiry now and again, then students will never develop proficiency with the skills the inquiry process teaches—that is, to become discerning and engaged citizens. If students experience inquiry every day, they develop the habits of mind that make these larger, nobler civic goals possible.

We agree with Ryan and teachers like him. In the section that follows, we walk through the defining characteristic of focused inquiry as driven by the tight coupling of content represented in sources with relevant skills and conceptual understanding, and highlight its key elements, noting where appropriate the differences between a focused and a structured blueprint.

Anatomy of a Focused Inquiry: How Should We Remember Columbus?

The Inquiry Design Model is rooted in the *blueprint*, a one-page representation of the common elements of inquiry-based practice—questions, tasks, and sources. Whether you are looking at the original or a focused adaptation, the blueprint offers a visual snapshot of an entire inquiry such that the individual components and the relationship among the components can all be seen at once. As such, the two blueprint forms have a similar structure: (1) compelling and supporting questions that frame and organize this inquiry; (2) formative and summative performance tasks that provide opportunities for students to demonstrate and apply their understandings; and (3) the disciplinary sources that allow students access to the relevant content as they practice disciplinary thinking and reasoning. (See Figure 5.4 on page 88.)

Questions

Questions are a foundational component of any form of inquiry, but in a focused inquiry the questions signal content that can elevate a specific skill or concept. For example, the compelling question "How should we remember Columbus?" calls on students to conduct an inquiry in the tradition of revisionist history, where they re-interpret the historical record by challenging dominant narratives about people or events of the past. In this inquiry, students examine Christopher Columbus, whose expeditions to the "new world" have traditionally been heralded in many U.S. history textbooks. Such a focus calls on students to practice understanding how perspectives change in history. This skill is highlighted in the C3 Framework indicator D2.His.5.6-8: Explain how and why perspectives of people have changed over time.

Throughout the inquiry, students examine Columbus's accomplishments through multiple lenses, including the perspectives of those who have been critical of his exploits and those who may see more value in his endeavors. We argue that understanding multiple perspectives is a key practice in historical thinking and a cornerstone of civic life, all of which makes the compelling question intellectually meaty and worth exploring.

Equally important is the student-friendly nature of a compelling question. This inquiry puts students in the historian's seat by asking them to sift through the historical record and evaluate it for themselves. By allowing students to practice the messy task of examining historical perspectives and interpretations, their voices

FIGURE 5.4: A FOCUSED INQUIRY BLUEPRINT ON RETHINKING CHRISTOPHER COLUMBUS

HOW SHOULD WE REMEMBER COLUMBUS?	
Illinois Social Science Standards	**SS.H.1.6-8.MC:** Use questions generated about individuals and groups to analyze why they, and the developments they shaped, are seen as historically significant.
Concept and Skill Focus	**Concept:** Colonialism. **Disciplinary Skill:** Perspective-Taking
Staging the Compelling Question	Examine two claims made about Christopher Columbus and, using prior knowledge, discuss the merits of each.

Supporting Question 1	Supporting Question 2
Understand and Assess	
Who was Columbus?	How has Columbus been remembered?
Formative Performance Task	**Formative Performance Task**
Complete a graphic organizer detailing what is known about Christopher Columbus.	Create a T-Chart with one side listing the ways in which Columbus has been remembered and one side listing the ways his image has been revisited by historians, educators, and governments.
Featured Sources	**Featured Sources**
Source A: Columbus reports on his first voyage, 1493 **Source B:** A map showing Columbus's four voyages to the Americas **Source C:** Excerpt from Bartholomew de las Casas's (1552) journal and engraving by Theodor de Bry (1552)	**Source A:** *Columbus Landing*, Vanderlyn painting (1842–47) **Source B:** History of Columbus Day, FDR Fireside Chat (1937) **Source C:** *In 1492*, poem that children are taught about Columbus **Source D:** Excerpt from James W. Loewen's book, *Lies My Teacher Told Me About Christopher Columbus: What Your History Books Got Wrong* (2014) **Source E:** Excerpt on Christopher Columbus from the text, *A People's History of the United States*, Howard Zinn (1980) **Source F:** Proclamations from State Governments replacing Columbus Day with Indigenous People's Day (2015)

Summative Performance Task	**ARGUMENT** How should we remember Columbus? Construct an argument consisting of a claim and counterclaim about how we should remember Columbus using the evidence encountered in this inquiry.
	ACT Read the assigned article and discuss how Illinois should reconcile the two holidays, Columbus Day and Indigenous People's Day. Write a letter to a lawmaker arguing whether you agree or disagree with Illinois' current position.

are heard and valued. What can be more compelling than to ask a student what she thinks instead of telling her what to think? As a result, we believe that the question "How should we remember Columbus?" not only satisfies the narrower criteria for a focused inquiry, but qualifies as a question that captures a student's imagination.

Focused inquiries retain the general direction of a compelling question, but tend to be narrower in the scope of content examined. Many IDM inquiries focus on broader topics or ideas (e.g., voting rights, the French Revolution, westward migration). The compelling questions in a focused inquiry typically explore a particular event, person, or concept. By design, these blueprints abbreviate the investigation with only 1-2 supporting questions. In the Rethinking Columbus inquiry, the supporting questions—Who was Columbus? and How has Columbus been remembered?—help students explore Columbus's actions and how those actions have been considered in art, politics, and history.

Although this inquiry focuses on a single historical actor, we think it is a good example of how teachers could revisit other controversial figures in history. For example, the compelling question architecture could stay in place (e.g., How should we remember _____?) even as the teacher changes the person under investigation (e.g., Thomas Jefferson, Eleanor Roosevelt, Malcolm X). When we delve deeply into the people of history and allow them to be fully human, neither heroes or villains, we acknowledge that history is a complex story made up of complicated actors and actions that are just as dynamic, multidimensional, and messy as humans are today.

Tasks

The heart of each inquiry, however, rests between two points—the compelling question and the summative argument. The formative work (i.e., supporting questions, formative performance tasks, and featured sources) is designed to prepare students to move constructively between those two points. In a focused inquiry, the argument might be truncated into a single claim and counter claim. Because the compelling question is narrower, the inquiry has only 1-2 formative performance tasks. The formative tasks follow through on the focus of the inquiry as well. If it is a skill that focuses the inquiry, students have the chance to practice with that skill in the formative tasks. If the focus is conceptual, then the formative task provides the chance for students to build their conceptual understandings.

In the Rethinking Columbus focused inquiry, the first formative performance task calls on students to complete a graphic organizer that outlines the achievements of Columbus, including his voyages and the mistreatment of the indigenous peoples he encountered. In the second formative performance task, students delve deeper into the many perspectives on Columbus's actions by creating a T-chart in which they list the ways Columbus has been remembered (e.g., paintings, holiday) and the ways our memory of him has been revisited by others including historians and policy makers. In this way, students are practicing the skill of understanding how and why perspectives of people have changed over time. This work, along with the background information gleaned in the exercise of staging the compelling question, allows students to move quickly to the summative argument task, which may include some of the claims below:

- We should remember Christopher Columbus as a brave explorer who, despite terrible odds, sailed across the Atlantic to discover the New World.

  – Evidence to support this claim can be found in several of the inquiries' sources including an excerpt from the journal of Columbus (1492), a map of his voyages, a painting of Columbus by John Vanderlyn (1842–47), and a fireside chat by President Franklin Delano Roosevelt (1937).

- Christopher Columbus did not "discover" America and instead should be remembered for enslaving and slaughtering many native people.

  – Evidence to support this claim can be found in several of the inquiries' sources including the excerpt from the journal of Columbus (1492), Bartholomew de las Casas's journal (1552), an etching by Theodor de Bry (1552), excerpts from history texts (e.g., James Loewen and Howard Zinn), and official proclamations from state governments that replace Columbus Day with Indigenous People's Day (2015).

Building on the summative argument task, students are able to extend their understandings creatively or civically through either an extension or a taking informed action task. The Rethinking Columbus focused inquiry asks students to investigate their state's stance toward Columbus Day and to write a letter to a lawmaker arguing a position about whether the state should rename or continue Columbus Day.

Sources

Sources complete the IDM model. Disciplinary sources offer access to content, while enabling the application of skills or conceptual understanding. It is here that IDM reveals the sometimes implied relationship between content in sources and skills and concepts. No successful student will be able to extract information and build content knowledge from sources without practicing skills and applying conceptual understanding. Sources require students to dig into the materials, build their content knowledge, and apply their analytical skills to move the inquiry forward.

One of the advantages of a focused inquiry is that it allows teachers to drill down on a particular skill. Sources in this focused inquiry provide an opportunity for students to practice with historical perspective taking by examining multiple sources that contrast views on Columbus as an explorer. For example, Figure 5.5 shows two of the sources within this inquiry that represent artistic depictions of Columbus.

Based on the journal entries of Bartholomew de las Casas, Theodor de Bry (1552) created an etching that depicts Columbus's men butchering the native peoples in order to subjugate them. This work stands in contrast to the painting by Vanderlyn (1842-47) that illustrates Columbus valiantly planting a flag for Spain while native people and the Spaniards fight in the background. Teacher-developed scaffolds can help students analyze these two artistic

FIGURE 5.5: TWO ARTISTS' RENDERINGS OF CHRISTOPHER COLUMBUS

Engraving by Theodor de Bry depicting the controversial account by Bartolomé de las Casas regarding the *Brevísima relación de la destrucción de las Indias* (A Short Account of the Destruction of the Indies), 1552.

Painting by John Vanderlyn depicting Columbus claiming possession of the New World in caravels, the Niña and the Pinta. Landing of Columbus (1842–47), U.S. Capitol Rotunda, Washington, D.C.

interpretations through questions such as: What is the perspective of the artist? What shaped the artists' depiction of Columbus? How do these interpretations compare and contrast? And, ultimately, how do I reconcile these interpretations when considering Columbus?

In thinking through these questions, students are practicing the skill of historical perspective taking. That skill allows students to understand how and why perspectives of people have changed over time, to consider the factors that have shaped ideas, attitudes, and beliefs, and to develop a sense of empathy with people in the past whose perspectives might be different from those of today. Ultimately, our aim is that students understand history as an interpretative discipline, not just a series of facts to be memorized and unquestioned.

Focused inquiries need to have sources that align closely with the outcomes planned for the inquiry. That's just good inquiry design. But that work demands that teachers make good decisions about what to include. No fluff here. Through focused inquiry, teachers direct students to the heart of the matter, carefully selecting, excerpting, and adapting sources so that their students are able to efficiently access the content they need to complete the inquiry tasks.

In this inquiry, the sources were curated so that the individual voices contrast with one another, providing multiple perspectives on Columbus. Each source sheds new light on this controversial figure by layering on complexity, while also showing change and continuity over time. For example, an astute student will note that Bartholomew de las Casas (1552) and Howard Zinn (1980)[6] provide a similar interpretation of Columbus even though their accounts were written almost 400 years apart. In contrast, FDR's 1937 fireside chat extolls the virtues and accomplishments of Columbus and establishes a national holiday in his honor, whereas more recently state holidays have been established to honor indigenous people whose lands were stolen by explorers like Columbus.

As students move through the sources, they learn to toggle between a variety of interpretations by artists, historians, educators, and others to learn how history is understood and revisited through time.

Design Considerations for a Focused Blueprint

As suggested earlier, the design process for focused inquiries is noteworthy. Although we follow the general IDM design process in developing a focused inquiry, it changes slightly to accommodate the unique focus on specific sources or a particular skill or concept. In the following sections, we discuss specific design considerations for the focused inquiry blueprint.

To animate the points below, we expand our discussion by providing additional examples of focused inquiry blueprints. These examples include: (1) An elementary-level blueprint featuring the compelling question, "What can Ruby Bridges teach us?" (2) A middle-level blueprint featuring the compelling question, "What does it mean to sacrifice?" And (3) A high school inquiry blueprint featuring the compelling question, "Did the attack on Pearl Harbor unify America?"

WE USE THE IDM DESIGN PROCESS WHEN BUILDING A FOCUSED INQUIRY. *It's just truncated a bit.* In developing a focused inquiry, we follow the design process by starting with framing an inquiry. We develop a narrower content angle that recognizes a tension in the content we want students to investigate, and we then tether the content to specific sources or a particular skill or concept that drives the content forward. From there we construct a compelling question that is both intellectually rigorous and relevant for students. We pressure test that compelling question with argument stems.

In the high school Pearl Harbor inquiry (see Figure 5.6 on page 94), the compelling question wraps tightly around a particular piece of content, the attack on Pearl Harbor. The focus of this inquiry takes shape in the choice of sources for delivering the content. This inquiry features sources from a unique collection of interviews with everyday people conducted during the days after the attack on Pearl Harbor. The sources provide a range of perspectives on the attack and the focus of the inquiry is aimed at supporting students as they make claims about whether the attack on Pearl Harbor unified America. From a design perspective, we pressure tested the compelling question with three argument stems to ensure that students can respond with an evidence-backed claim:

- Many Americans felt the attack on Pearl Harbor was a galvanizing event that unified Americans in entering the war.

- Some Americans felt the war at home against anti-Semitism and Jim Crow laws was more significant than the war abroad.

- Some Americans wanted to join the war effort long before the attack on Pearl Harbor.

Each of these claims could be supported with information from the sources that focus this inquiry. We checked and double checked that as we moved through the design process ensuring that students could ultimately make evidence-based arguments. It is important to note that the compelling question, the argument stems, and the sources are intentionally limited in scope. Instead of asking, "Was World War II an example of a just war?" we intentionally limit the focused inquiry to just one pivotal event during the larger war. The need to narrow is inherent in a focused inquiry and ultimately impacts all aspects of the inquiry.

FIGURE 5.6: A FOCUSED INQUIRY BLUEPRINT ON PEARL HARBOR

DID THE ATTACK ON PEARL HARBOR UNIFY AMERICA?

New York State Social Studies (NYSSS) Framework Key Idea(s)	**11.8. WORLD WAR II (1935 – 1945):** The participation of the United States in World War II was a transformative event for the nation and its role in the world.
Inquiry Focus: NYSSS Framework Key Practice(s)	**Gathering, Using, and Interpreting Evidence:** Make inferences and draw conclusions from evidence. **Comparison and Contextualization:** Identify, compare, and evaluate multiple perspectives on a given historical experience.
Staging the Compelling Question	Listen to FDR's Day of Infamy Speech and read the description of the Library of Congress collection, *After the Day of Infamy: "Man-on-the-Street" Interviews Following the Attack on Pearl Harbor*. Predict what people across the country said about going to war with Japan.

Supporting Question 1

What did people say about American involvement at the beginning of the war?

Formative Performance Task

Create a graphic organizer that categorizes the different reactions that everyday Americans had to the attack on Pearl Harbor.

Featured Sources

Source A: "Man-on-the-Street," New York, New York, December 8, 1941

Source B: "Dear Mr. President," New York, New York, January or February 1942

Source C: "Man-on-the-Street," Austin, Texas, December 9, 1941

Source D: "Man-on-the-Street," Nashville, Tennessee, December 1941

Source E: "Dear Mr. President," New York, New York, January or February 1942

Source F: "Dear Mr. President," Minneapolis, Minnesota, January or February 1942

Summative Performance Task	**ARGUMENT** Did the attack on Pearl Harbor unify America? Construct a claim and a counterclaim that address the compelling question using historical evidence.
	EXTENSION Examine the story of Pearl Harbor told by a history textbook and propose revisions based on the perspectives represented in the featured sources.

Once we have that curricular foundation in place, we begin filling an inquiry by developing 1-2 supporting questions that enable students to analyze the sets of sources selected to help them develop their evidence-based arguments. Formative performance tasks typically have students sorting information from sources by perspectives on an event, person, or issue. This approach is evident in the focused inquiry on Pearl Harbor, where students are working through six sources that demonstrate the varied opinions of Americans and their reactions to the attack. Students are asked to sort the information they glean from the sources and to chart it on a graphic organizer.

Finally, we finish the inquiry design with an exercise for Staging the Compelling Question along with an opportunity for Extension or Taking Informed Action. When designing these components, we take time into consideration and so these focused blueprints are less elaborate than they might be for a structured inquiry. For example, in the focused inquiry on Pearl Harbor, teachers can stage the compelling question by asking students to listen to FDR's Day of Infamy Speech and then read the introduction to the source collection they are investigating. Students can take informed action by reading a textbook account of the Pearl Harbor attack and determining its accuracy and, if necessary, proposing revisions to the text.

The key to designing a focused inquiry is clear—rework the elements of inquiry with an eye for time. Clarity around a focus helps teachers cut the curricular clutter from the inquiry, while retaining its essential elements. As you do this, remember Picasso's bull from Chapter 2 and the move toward the essence of inquiry!

MORE OFTEN THAN NOT, FOCUSED INQUIRIES ARE INSPIRED BY A CLEARLY FOCUSED TOPIC. The inspiration for a focused inquiry can come from any direction—e.g., a topic you have wanted to explore, but haven't found time for or an activity that you think would engage your students. Our experience tells us, however, that focused inquiries are often inspired by a clearly focused topic. Sometimes it is a set of sources that talk to one another in some important way such as the sources in the Pearl Harbor inquiry. Other times it may be a single source. The sources could unfold a historical narrative about a person, they could provide differing perspectives on an event, or they may even provide multiple examples of a case study.

The inspiration for the elementary-focused inquiry on Ruby Bridges (see Figure 5.7 on page 96) was an award-winning trade book, *Through My Eyes* by Ruby Bridges.[7] In this powerful narrative,

WHAT CAN RUBY BRIDGES TEACH US?

Syracuse City Curriculum Key Idea	**3.4:** Each community or culture has a unique history, including heroic figures, traditions, and holidays. **3.7:** Governments in communities and countries around the world have the authority to make and the power to enforce laws. The role of the citizen within these communities or countries varies across different types of governments
Concept and Skill Focus	**Concept:** Non-Violent Resistance. **Disciplinary Skill:** Gathering information from sources
Staging the Compelling Question	Watch the video clip of Ruby Bridges' first day of school, from the movie *Ruby Bridges,* to find out how she was treated unfairly. Lead a class discussion of Ruby's experiences on her first day of school and if and how they were unfair.

Supporting Question 1	Supporting Question 2
What motivated Ruby Bridges to stand up?	What did Ruby Bridges do?
Formative Performance Task	**Formative Performance Task**
Complete section of the graphic organizer labeled "Actions Ruby Bridges took".	Complete section of the graphic organizer labeled "Reasons Ruby Bridges stood up".
Featured Sources	**Featured Sources**
Source A: *Through My Eyes*, a trade book on Ruby Bridges	**Source A:** *Through My Eyes*, a trade book on Ruby Bridges **Source B:** Photographs of Jim Crow Era Segregation **Source C:** Photographs of segregated classrooms

Summative Performance Task	**ARGUMENT** Construct an argument (e.g., graphic) about what Ruby Bridges can teach us. **EXTENSION** Research where Ruby Bridges is now and her lasting legacy on public education.

Bridges tells her story of being the first black child to attend a New Orleans public elementary school. The book represents a first-person oral history of the experience alongside original photographs and documents from the time, including newspaper accounts and sidebar statements from people who knew Bridges at the time. Together these documents inspired the compelling question, "What can Ruby Bridges teach us?"

Those teachers wanting to build a focused inquiry may find inspiration with a trade book or with a primary source set from the Digital Public Library of America (**https://dp.la/primary-source-sets**) or the Library of Congress (**http://www.loc.gov/teachers/classroommaterials/primarysourcesets/**). Many museums are beginning to organize their digital collections into source sets for teachers and so offer a great way to begin the inquiry design process.

TEACHERS MAY WANT TO STACK OR LOOP FOCUSED INQUIRIES SO THAT STUDENTS CAN HAVE REPEATED PRACTICE OF A SKILL OR CONCEPT. One of the advantages of a focused inquiry is that it helps a teacher target a particular skill or concept that students need to practice. We know that the development of any skill or conceptual understanding takes repeated exposure and practice because mastery of a skill or idea can be slippery or elusive.[8]

Teachers could be deliberate in their use of focused inquiry to reinforce skill or concept development. For example, a teacher may want students to master the following skill within the C3 Framework indicator D2.His.5.6-8: Explain how and why perspectives of people have changed over time.

A teacher using the Columbus inquiry might loop the skill of identifying and analyzing multiple perspectives on a controversial figure by doing a series of inquiries across a course examining how we should remember Andrew Jackson, Elizabeth Cady Stanton, or Barack Obama. Included within each focused inquiry would be various and conflicting depictions of the historical figure. Although all types of inquiries could be used to loop skills and ideas, focused inquiries are well-positioned to do this more often.

In another middle school inquiry with the compelling question, "What does it mean to sacrifice?" students examine the commonalities among soldiers asked to go to war (See Figure 5.8). Combing past and contemporary oral histories on the Korean War, students consider how soldiers' perspectives of the war changed over time. Although this inquiry has a different content focus, it shares the same objective as the Rethinking Columbus inquiry by asking students to explore how and why perspectives of people change over time.

In the section that follows the blueprint (Figure 5.8 on page 98), we summarize the instructional advantages of a focused inquiry, while noting its challenges.

FIGURE 5.8: A FOCUSED INQUIRY BLUEPRINT ON SACRIFICE DURING THE KOREAN WAR

WHAT DOES IT MEAN TO SACRIFICE?	
C3 Framework Indicator	D2.His.3.6-8. Use questions generated about individuals and groups to analyze why they, and the developments they shaped, are seen as historically significant. D2.His.5.6-8. Explain how and why perspectives of people have changed over time.
Concept and Skill Focus	**Concept:** Impact of War **Skill:** Change over time
Staging the Compelling Question	Discuss the historical significance of individual and group sacrifice in times of conflict and war.

Supporting Question 1	Supporting Question 2
How did soldiers sacrifice during the war?	How did Koreans sacrifice during the war?
Formative Performance Task	**Formative Performance Task**
Make a list of examples of the sacrifices of soldiers in the Korean War?	Write a paragraph about the sacrifices of Koreans in the Korean War.
Featured Sources	**Featured Sources**
Source A: Chapter from the Korean War Legacy Project, "POW Experience" Source B: Personal narrative by Bob Mitchell, a Marine Corps veteran, on his extensive front-line combat experience Source C: Personal narrative by Fred Liddell, Korean War veteran, on his capture by Chinese troops in 1951 Source D: Link to the Korean War Legacy Project's Memory Bank to search for other veteran interviews describing soldiers' sacrifices	Source A: Chapter from the Korean War Legacy Project, "The Human Experience" Source B: Personal narrative of Donald J. Zoeller, 140th Anti-Aircraft Battalion, on his experiences near the main line of resistance (MLR) Source C: Personal narrative of Clarence Jerke, 2nd Infantry Division Headquarters Battery, on his work maintaining communications lines behind enemy lines Source D: Photograph of Seoul, October 18, 1950; also link to the Korean War Legacy Project's Memory Bank to search for additional photographs of and veteran interviews about Koreans' sacrifices

Summative Performance Task	**ARGUMENT** "What does it mean to sacrifice?" Construct an argument (e.g., detailed outline, poster, or essay) that discusses the compelling question using specific claims and relevant evidence from the sources provided, as well as one other source, while acknowledging competing views.
	EXTENSION Using the argument as a foundation, engage in small-group brainstorming to create an original poem or song responding to the compelling question, "What does it mean to sacrifice?"
Taking Informed Action	**UNDERSTAND** Examine the historical significance of sacrifices made by individuals and groups during a current or recent conflict or war.
	ASSESS Determine some ways the stories of soldiers fighting abroad might be shared in the community.
	ACT Organize a school- or community-wide effort to share poems or songs of appreciation from students with local veterans' associations.

Affordances and Constraints of a Focused Inquiry

Abbreviating inquiry into a 1-2 day lesson means that some ideas are going to be left on the cutting room floor. But, that is true for curriculum in general. Teachers must make decisions about what to teach within the allotted time for social studies. Although content breadth is an opportunity cost of inquiry, it is important to remember what students gain in the process of inquiry. When students work with the elements of inquiry, they wrestle with important questions, mine disciplinary sources for answers and insights, craft evidence-based claims/counterclaims, and then communicate their conclusions expressively or civically. Given a chance to do this process repeatedly, students become more proficient at it, helping us achieve the goals set out in the C3 Framework.

In the table below, we summarize the instructional affordances and constraints of a focused Inquiry.

TABLE 5.3: INSTRUCTIONAL AFFORDANCES AND CONSTRAINTS OF A FOCUSED INQUIRY

FOCUSED INQUIRY	
Instructional Affordances	Instructional Constraints
Saves time over more structured inquiry experiences	Requires prioritization of content and that teachers trade content breadth for depth
Allows for focused skill development and a deep dive into specific content	Reduces the time for intellectual wandering and could feel a bit prescribed or formulaic without balancing other kinds of inquiry
Provides teachers with an efficient approach to loop inquiry into a content-heavy curriculum	

Conclusion

In the next two chapters, we reimagine the blueprint to give teachers curricular spaces that include student research, including the Guided and Self-Directed blueprints.

ENDNOTES

1. C. Counsell, "Historical Knowledge and Historical Skills: The Distracting Dichotomy," in J. Arthur & R. Phillips (Eds.), *Issues in History Teaching* (London: Routledge, 2000).

2. C. Gewertz, "New Social Studies Framework Aims to Guide Standards," *Education Week* 33, no. 5 (September 17, 2013), 8. Retrieved from **https://www.edweek.org/ew/articles/2013/09/17/05socialstudies.h33.html**.

3. National Council for the Social Studies (NCSS), *College, Career, and Civic Life (C3) Framework for Social Studies State Standards* (Silver Spring, MD: NCSS, 2013).

4. J. Lee and K. Swan, "Is the Common Core Good for Social Studies? Yes, But... " *Social Education*, 77, no. 6 (November-December 2013), 327-330.

5. S.G. Grant, K. Swan and J. Lee, *Inquiry-Based Practice in Social Studies Education: The Inquiry Design Model* (New York: Routledge and C3Teachers, 2017); K. Swan, J. Lee and S.G. Grant, *Inquiry Design Model: Building Inquiries in Social Studies* (Silver Spring, MD: National Council for the Social Studies and C3 Teachers, 2018).

6. Howard Zinn, *A People's History of the United States* (New York: Harper and Row, 1980).

7. R. Bridges and M. Lundell, *Through My Eyes* (New York: Scholastic Press, 2009).

8. S.G. Grant, "Understanding What Children Know about History: Exploring the Representation and Testing Dilemmas," *Social Studies Research and Practice* 2, no. 2(2007), 196-208. Available on-line at http://www.socstrp.org.

CHAPTER 6

Guided Inquiry: Scaffolding Student Research in an Inquiry

One conversation that we have had consistently with teacher colleagues is about student research and agency within an inquiry. An exchange that regularly occurs during our sessions starts with a set of questions from teachers that look something like this:

Questions, tasks, and sources as the foundation of inquiry...yep!
A one-page blueprint to organize the inquiry...makes sense to me!

But...

When do students learn how to research?
When do they learn how to find sources around a topic?
When do students acquire strategies for finding reliable and credible information?

I thought inquiry generally and social studies specifically helps students learn how to be citizens and scholars who can find important information independently!

Am I missing something?

And we always respond with, "nope—you're not missing a thing!" We could not agree more that students need to learn how to conduct research and find credible information as they answer compelling and supporting questions. And, ultimately, students need the skills to do this work independently. Not only is research an essential skill for all college students and workers, it is foundational for an engaged and informed citizenry.

So, how does IDM help build students' capacity for disciplinary research? This is where *guided inquiry* can help. Guided inquiry offers students opportunities to research answers to supporting questions within a teacher-developed inquiry. During the inquiry, students learn how to locate credible sources that help answer one or more supporting questions. In this way, the guided inquiry blueprints provide a supportive research experience.

In this chapter, we describe the unique function of a guided inquiry in helping students learn to research and find useful sources within an inquiry. We use a guided inquiry blueprint on child activism to examine the architecture of questions, tasks, and sources and the nested opportunities for student research. Then, we look at the design and instructional considerations for developing and teaching a guided inquiry. We conclude the chapter by discussing the instructional affordances and constraints teachers face when employing this type of inquiry experience.

Scaffolding Inquiry

In order to understand the characteristics of a guided inquiry blueprint, it is important to start with the overall goal of the IDM. Regardless of type, all IDM blueprints (e.g., focused, structured, embedded-action, guided, or student-directed) offer a curricular scaffold for inquiry. Before we delve too deeply into the scaffolds of a guided inquiry, let's take a moment to establish a language for discussing scaffolds.

Generally speaking, scaffolds are pedagogical supports that assist students in the learning process.[1] One theory of scaffolding includes a delineation between *hard* and *soft* scaffolds.[2] Hard scaffolds are those supports that a teacher designs in advance of instruction to help students with a learning task. In contrast, soft scaffolds occur during the instruction when a teacher notices students struggling with the learning task. In this instance, that teacher might intervene with some direct instructional tasks to help students overcome their content and/or skill challenges. In both hard and soft varieties, the idea of "expert scaffolding"[3] is at work—that is, an expert or teacher is assisting a novice or student.

Through inquiry-based practice, teachers work with hard scaffolds to structure the inquiry experiences of students. These hard scaffolds come in two forms: curricular and instructional. *Curricular* scaffolds help to break down the content of an inquiry into reasonable chunks of information and then sequence those chunks in a way that provides a coherent learning experience. For example, one curricular scaffold involves unpacking the compelling question so it is accessible for students. We do this in several ways. First, the process of staging the compelling question allows students to explore the major concepts inherent in the compelling question. Inquiry designers further unpack the compelling question by creating supporting questions that divide the content of the inquiry into reasonable chunks of information. Then, the supporting questions are sequenced across the blueprint so that the content unfolds in a logical way for students. In these ways, the unique elements of the blueprint work as a curricular scaffold for students learning how to do disciplined inquiry.

Another curricular scaffold within the blueprint involves preparing students for the summative argument task. Inquiry designers create a series of formative performance tasks that allow students to build the requisite knowledge and to practice the discrete skills of argumentation before they tackle the summative argument. This formative work could ask students to summarize information from a source, to compare and contrast multiple sources, and/or to develop an evidence-based claim. All of these design elements provide curricular support for students learning to construct evidence-based arguments.

Curricular scaffolds are hard-wired into the blueprint, whereas *instructional* scaffolds are additional hard scaffolds that teachers put in place to make disciplinary practices more intuitive for students. Most evident in guided inquiries, there is a need for teachers to create instructional scaffolds (e.g., graphic organizers) to support students in categorizing information and in thinking their ways through sources. In the sections below, we walk through a number of these instructional scaffolds created specifically for the inquiries we highlight. Teachers can customize these instructional scaffolds to wrap tightly around the content and skills of the inquiry, in contrast with more generic instructional scaffolds or source heuristics (e.g., APPARTS—Author, Place and time, Prior Knowledge, Audience, Reasoning, The main idea, Significance; or SCIM-C—Summarizing, Contextualizing, Inferring, Monitoring, and Corroborating).

IDM stays mostly silent on teachers' soft scaffolding of inquiry instruction. These scaffolds are classroom- and student-dependent; as teachers implement their inquiries, they keep track of their students' strengths and weaknesses and construct scaffolds to address the latter. Understanding when and how and why teachers use instructional scaffolds is important so we are collecting examples of these learning experiences, which we hope to chronicle in an upcoming book.[4]

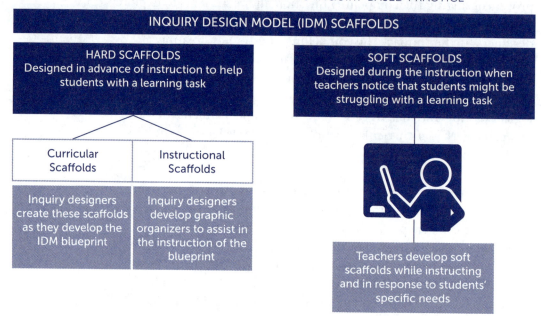

Figure 6.1 portrays the ways that hard and soft scaffolds for IDM and the classroom can be used.

These various scaffolds allow us to discuss the aims of inquiry-based practice as a whole and to distinguish the defining characters of each one. In the following section, we introduce a guided inquiry blueprint that features both curricular and instructional hard scaffolds that support independent student research.*

Characteristics of a Guided Inquiry

A guided inquiry blueprint is designed so that students can practice being independent in the research process. In these blueprints, teachers construct the compelling and supporting questions as well as the corresponding formative and summative tasks. (See Table 6.1.) But the teacher also crafts at least one independent research opportunity within the formative work. Within that research experience, students might be asked to find the sources that would help answer the supporting question.

---

* As part of the New York Toolkit Project (https://www.engageny.org/resource/new-york-state-k-12-social-studies-resource-toolkit), inquiry writers developed a set of 12 annotated inquiries, one per grade level, that articulate both the curricular and instructional scaffolds that could be included in an inquiry. Readers wanting to access those inquiries could consult Appendix A at the end of this chapter, which provides a table of these annotated inquiries.

TABLE 6.1: ELEMENTS OF A GUIDED INQUIRY

GUIDED INQUIRY	
Description	The teacher develops the inquiry, but there are dedicated spaces in the formative work for students to conduct independent research.
Role of Teacher and/or Student in Blueprint Development	Teacher and student-developed
Questions	The teacher develops the questions, but there are opportunities in the formative work for students to conduct independent research.
Tasks	The teacher develops summative and formative tasks, but some of the formative tasks are structured so that students are researching a supporting question.
Sources	The teacher selects some sources and students select some sources as they relate to the research opportunity.
Instructional Time	5-10 days

It is within the supporting question or, in some cases, multiple supporting questions, that teachers can remove a curricular scaffold from the inquiry—the teacher-selected featured sources. In allowing students to select appropriate sources to answer the supporting question, teachers are able to create agency for students within a structured inquiry process. Doing so requires additional instructional scaffolds, but we think that is a natural part of teaching. As educators, we are always trying to understand where our students are and then responding with scaffolds tailored to support their development as independent learners.

It is worth noting that more student autonomy is likely going to mean additional time on the instructional clock. We find that guided inquiries demand between five to ten instructional days—longer than the instructional time for either a focused inquiry or most structured ones. In the section that follows, we walk through an elementary-level guided inquiry on childhood activism and highlight its key elements, noting where appropriate the differences between it and the focused and structured blueprints.

Anatomy of a Guided Inquiry: How Do Children Make History?

Like the structured and focused inquiry blueprints, the guided inquiry blueprint is a one-page visual representation of the questions, tasks, and sources that define an inquiry. There are compelling and supporting questions, formative and summative performance tasks, and selected disciplinary sources that aid students in answering the inquiry's questions. (See Figure 6.2 on page 106). In the sections that follow, we walk through these elements.

FIGURE 6.2: A GUIDED INQUIRY BLUEPRINT ON CHILDHOOD ACTIVISM

HOW DO CHILDREN MAKE HISTORY?	
Syracuse City Curriculum Key Ideas	**3.6:** Communities from around the world interact with other people and communities and exchange cultural ideas and practices. **3.7:** Governments in communities and countries around the world have the authority to make and the power to enforce laws. The role of the citizen within these communities or countries varies across different types of governments.
Staging the Compelling Question	Read Malala Yousafzai's story from the book *Never Too Young*. Determine Malala's motivations, actions, and challenges she faced in making history.

Supporting Question 1	Supporting Question 2	Supporting Question 3	Supporting Question 4
Guided Research	**Guided Research**	**Guided Research**	**Guided Research**
What activist am I going to investigate?	What reasons motivated my activist?	What did my activist do?	What challenges did my activist face?
Formative Performance Task	**Formative Performance Task**	**Formative Performance Task**	**Formative Performance Task**
Complete the research organizer, "Which activist will I research?"	Complete the "motivations" column on the research organizer.	Complete the "actions" column on the research organizer.	Complete the "challenges faced" column on the research organizer.
Featured Sources	**Featured Sources**	**Featured Sources**	**Featured Sources**
Source A: *Never Too Young*	**Source A:** *Never Too Young* *Students select one to two additional sources to support their research.*	**Source A:** *Never Too Young* *Students select one to two additional sources to support their research.*	**Source A:** *Never Too Young* *Students select one to two additional sources to support their research.*

Summative Performance Task	**ARGUMENT** Construct an argument about your chosen activist and how and why he or she made history.
	EXTENSION Create a poster about your activist and present it to the class.

Questions

Guided inquiry begins with a compelling question that provides the starting place for the inquiry. As with all inquiry blueprints, compelling questions should be both academically rigorous and relevant to students. In the guided inquiry above, the compelling question "How do children make history?" asks students to investigate children around the world who became change agents by working on problematic issues.

Is this question compelling? We think so. Studying history means examining the historical record to understand how people lived in the past, what challenges they faced, and how they overcame those challenges. History books are filled with individuals who stood up and stood out, capturing the attention of historians who determined that those actions are historically significant. Students in this inquiry examine children who have crossed the threshold of being historically significant in that they pivoted through history with a meaningful action. In this way, the question is inherently rigorous and worthy of students' time and attention.

We also think this investigation appeals to students. Most history lessons focus on adults who changed history—think Alexander the Great, Harriet Beecher Stowe, Mahatma Gandhi, and Catherine the Great. By looking at turning points brought on by children, students can see that they, too, can make history—even in third grade! Within the inquiry, students examine Malala Yousafzai, Helen Keller, Nkosi Johnson, and others whose contributions unfold on the pages of history.

The supporting questions in this inquiry serve as a curricular scaffold for student research. They begin with the first supporting question, which asks, "What activist am I going to investigate?" Students working through this inquiry select a child activist from a list compiled using the trade book, *Never Too Young! 50 Unstoppable Kids Who Made a Difference*.[5] After selecting their activists, the supporting questions create a useful structure for students' investigations:

- What reasons motivated this activist?

- What did the activist do?

- What challenges did the activist face?

Through these questions, students examine the child activists' motivations and actions, and the challenges they faced. As such, the supporting question sequence helps to delineate and clarify a robust study into the activists' lives and contributions. Taken together, the four supporting questions offer a logical progression and a common structure as students select and then research their individual activists.

Tasks

Like structured and focused inquiries, a guided inquiry is designed so that students answer the compelling question in the form of a summative argument. The formative performance tasks allow students a space to build up their content knowledge and to practice argumentation skills.

The task of staging the compelling question plays an important role in establishing this inquiry. We sometimes refer to the staging exercise as the first formative task because it allows students to begin playing with the big ideas embedded within the compelling question. The staging exercise in the child activism inquiry does this and more. To stage this inquiry, students read Malala Yousafzai's story from the book *Never Too Young: 50 Unstoppable Kids Who Made a Difference.*[6] Students work collaboratively with the teacher to determine Malala's motivations and actions, and the challenges she faced when elevating the awareness of girls' rights to an education. This exercise provides students (individually or with a partner) with an opportunity to practice collectively what they will be doing within the inquiry and to foreshadow the key categories of their research efforts. In this way, the staging exercise provides an important curricular scaffold in the guided inquiry process.

With Malala as the guiding example, students then tackle the first formative performance task by selecting a child activist. Because this is an elementary-level inquiry, teachers might use a research organizer (an instructional scaffold) to support students as they complete the first formative performance task. (See Figure 6.3.)

FIGURE 6.3: RESEARCH ORGANIZER FOR FORMATIVE PERFORMATIVE TASK 1 OF THE INQUIRY, "HOW DO CHILDREN MAKE HISTORY?"

I am going to research _____.

I chose _____

because _____.

The next three formative performance tasks ask students to work through three columns using another instructional scaffold, a graphic organizer, which enables them to document the motivations and actions of their activists, and the challenges they faced. Figure 6.4 illustrates a version of graphic organizer a teacher might develop.

The summative argument task asks students to create a graphic representation, in this case a poster, of how their activists changed history in their community, state, or nation. On their posters, students pull from the formative performance tasks to describe what their activists did, the reasons for their activism, and the challenges they faced. Students' arguments will vary depending on the category or activist chosen, but could include something like the following:

COMPELLING QUESTION: HOW DO CHILDREN MAKE HISTORY?		
Activist's Name:		
Motivations	Actions	Challenges

- *Children make history fighting for equal education for girls in societies where girls face challenges in going to school.*

  – Evidence for this argument: Malala Yousafzai made history by speaking for the rights of girls to have an education even after she was attacked for attending school.

- *Children make history by making sure people have clean water to drink.*

  – Evidence for this argument: Ryan Hreljac raises money to build wells in a developing country so more people have clean and safe water to drink.

- *Children make history by inventing new products that can save people's lives.*

  – Evidence for this argument: Jack Andraka made history by inventing a new way to detect cancer earlier so people can receive treatment sooner.

- *Children make history by teaching and helping others.*

  – Evidence for this argument: Katie Stagliono made history by teaching others about farming and donating her crops to people in need.

Building on the summative argument task, students are able to extend their understandings by presenting their posters to the class and engaging in a class discussion about making societal change.

Sources

Sources are foundational to the IDM model and are selected by the teacher in both the structured and focused blueprints. By contrast, guided inquiry blueprints provide space for students to select some of the sources necessary to help them answer the supporting questions.

In this inquiry, the trade book *Never Too Young: 50 Unstoppable Kids Who Made a Difference* is a foundational source for all the supporting questions.[7] The book is separated into short biographical sketches of 50 children who changed history. Each person is represented by an image, an attributed quote, and a story about her or his life and contributions. For example, the biographical sketch of Yash Gupta presents an image of Yash and the quote "Kids are passionate and can make a difference. It's just a matter of finding out what you care about and focusing on that." The story describes how Yash realized that millions of people throw away perfectly good pairs of eyeglasses every year when they get new prescriptions. At the same time, millions of children who need eyeglasses but cannot afford them are not able to learn at school because of their lack of glasses. Yash came up with a plan for a non-profit organization that would collect eyeglasses and distribute them to children in need throughout the world. The 49 other young people featured in the book are drawn from different countries and historical eras, and have all made significant achievements by the age of 18. Students engaged in the inquiry "How do children make history?" will find a wide range of possibilities in this book as they select an activist to study.

Students use *Never Too Young* as the starting place for their investigations. For the remainder of the inquiry, they are asked to select one to two additional sources to support their research. They are expected to find sources that help them understand their activists' motivations and actions, and the challenges they faced as outlined in the formative performance tasks.

Teachers interested in this type of inquiry will need to think about where students can look for sources. For example, they should think about whether students will visit the media center and/or whether they will use the Internet, and, if so, which sites are appropriate. Beyond those initial questions of where and how students may find sources, teachers need to think about two more design issues—how to help their students assess the credibility of their found sources and how they access the information within the sources that they find so that they can answer the supporting questions.

Where one scaffold comes down, invariably other scaffolds may need to be erected to assist students in the research process. Teachers might call on other educators (e.g., media specialists) to assist them in these research endeavors. Although this type of inquiry requires some additional time and energy, we think that the goal of students learning to research independently makes this blueprint adaptation a worthwhile addition to the IDM.

Design Considerations for a Guided Blueprint

When we build guided inquiries, we follow the 10-step IDM design process articulated in our last book, *Inquiry Design Model: Building Inquiries for the Social Studies Classroom.*[8] We give particular attention to students finding featured sources in the formative work and the curricular scaffolds (e.g., supporting questions, formative performance tasks) that can be created to make those research experiences productive. In the following sections, we discuss additional instructional scaffolds that are design considerations for the guided inquiry blueprint.

To animate the points below, we expand our discussion by providing additional examples of guided inquiry blueprints. These additional examples include: (1) a high school blueprint featuring the compelling question, "What made non-violent protest effective during the Civil Rights Movement?" and (2) a middle school blueprint featuring the compelling question, "What do the pyramids tell us about the past?"

MODEL RESEARCH EXPERIENCES FOR STUDENTS BEFORE STUDENTS RESEARCH INDEPENDENTLY. In developing a guided inquiry, we think that practice makes perfect. In the child activism inquiry, we had students practice understanding the significance of child activists beginning with the task of staging the compelling question. In other inquiries, we might build this guided practice into the formative work. For example, in the high school inquiry "What made non-violent protest effective during the Civil Rights Movement?"students work as a whole group through the first supporting question that focuses their study of the non-violent protest by the individuals who participated in the Greensboro Sit-In. Presumably, a teacher would play an active role in teaching this important event and modeling how to work through the sources that enable students to investigate the supporting question, "What was the impact of the Greensboro Sit-In Protest?" (See Figure 6.5 on page 112.)

FIGURE 6.5: A GUIDED INQUIRY BLUEPRINT ON CIVIL RIGHTS

WHAT MADE NONVIOLENT PROTEST EFFECTIVE DURING THE CIVIL RIGHTS MOVEMENT?

New York State Social Studies Framework Key Ideas & Practices	**11.10 SOCIAL AND ECONOMIC CHANGE/DOMESTIC ISSUES (1945 – PRESENT):** Racial, gender, and socioeconomic inequalities were addressed by individuals, groups, and organizations. Varying political philosophies prompted debates over the role of federal government in regulating the economy and providing a social safety net. ☑ **Gathering, Using, and Interpreting Evidence** ☑ **Chronological Reasoning and Causation**
Staging the Compelling Question	Discuss the recent die-in protests and the extent to which they are an effective form of nonviolent direct-action protest.

Supporting Question 1	Supporting Question 2	Supporting Question 3
	Guided Student Research	Independent Student Research
What was the impact of the Greensboro sit-in protest?	What made the Montgomery bus boycott, the Birmingham campaign, and the Selma to Montgomery marches effective?	How did others use nonviolence effectively during the civil rights movement?
Formative Performance Task	**Formative Performance Task**	**Formative Performance Task**
Create a cause-and-effect diagram that demonstrates the impact of the sit-in protest by the Greensboro Four.	Detail the impacts of a range of actors and the actions they took to make the efforts effective.	Research the impact of a range of actors and the effective nonviolent direct actions they used in events during the civil rights movement.
Featured Sources	**Featured Sources**	**Featured Sources**
Source A: Photograph of the Greensboro Four **Source B:** *Join the Student Sit-Ins* **Source C:** "1960: Sitting Down to Take a Stand"	**Sources A–D:** Source packet on the Montgomery bus boycott **Sources A–D:** Source packet on the Birmingham campaign **Sources A–E:** Source packet on the Selma to Montgomery marches	**Source A:** To be determined by students; see possible resources in the Events for Research table (Figure 6.6)

Summative Performance Task	**ARGUMENT** What made nonviolent protest effective during the civil rights movement? Construct an argument (e.g., detailed outline, poster, or essay) using specific claims and relevant evidence from historical sources. Express these arguments by creating a monument or memorial for nonviolent heroes of the civil rights movement and provide a rationale for its design.
	EXTENSION Discuss the following: If the country were to build a monument or memorial (e.g., Mount Rushmore or the Vietnam War Memorial) for nonviolent heroes of the civil rights movement, what type of monument should it be and who, if anyone, should be on it?
Taking Informed Action	**UNDERSTAND** Examine several oral history archives. Focus on archives that feature individuals who participated in nonviolent protests within the civil rights movement.
	ASSESS Discuss the limitations of oral history and note its contribution to our understanding of the past.
	ACT Create an oral history archive of individuals who participated in or witnessed a nonviolent direct-action protest.

In the second supporting question, the inquiry provides space for students to have a guided research experience through which they might be placed into three groups, each of which focuses on either the Montgomery Bus Boycott, the Birmingham Bus Boycott, or the Selma to Montgomery marches. Students then work from provided source packets to detail the impact that the individuals involved had on the larger Civil Rights Movement.

These two experiences set the stage for the third supporting question, which asks students to engage in an independent research experience investigating others who impacted the movement through non-violent means. By having students practice the research experience with the teacher and then in small groups, teachers are able to build their students' capacity for and success with independent research. Teachers will want to think about these strategic scaffolds as they build guided inquiries.

DON'T BE AFRAID TO LIMIT THE SCOPE OF THE RESEARCH. In both of the inquiries featured in this chapter thus far, the independent research experience has been bounded in terms of content. For example, in the elementary-level child activism inquiry, we limited the research to a list of child activists selected from a single text. In the high school civil rights inquiry, we designed the culminating research experience to include four events—the Freedom Rides, the March on Washington, the Freedom Summer, and the Chicago Freedom Movement. For each event, we provided between 5 and 10 names of individuals involved in the event, as well as between 4 and 6 possible online sources. For example, the table below (Figure 6.6) features one event, five people, one organization, and four web sites that students could use to begin their research.

FIGURE 6.6: AN EXAMPLE OF LIMITING THE SCOPE OF RESEARCH THROUGH GUIDED EXAMPLES

EVENTS FOR RESEARCH		
Event	People/Organization	Possible Web Sources
Freedom Rides	Genevieve Hughes Houghton	"Freedom Riders" episode of *American Experience*, PBS website: http://www.pbs.org/wgbh/americanexperience/freedomriders/
	Robert Kennedy	"Freedom Rides" encyclopedia entry, Martin Luther King and the Global Freedom Struggle, The Martin Luther King, Jr. Research and Education Institute, Stanford University: http://mlk-kpp01.stanford.edu/index.php/encyclopedia/encyclopedia/enc_freedom_rides/
	James Lawson	
	Diane Nash	
	James Peck	Marian Smith Holmes, "The Freedom Riders, Then and Now," *Smithsonian Magazine*, February 2009: http://www.smithsonianmag.com/history/the-freedom-riders-then-and-now-45351758/
	Congress of Racial Equality (CORE)	
		Freedom Riders Oral Histories, Archives and Special Collections, University of Mississippi Libraries: http://clio.lib.olemiss.edu/cdm/landingpage/collection/freeriders/

We followed this same structure for a middle school inquiry where students investigate the compelling question, "What do the pyramids tell us about the past?" They begin as a group studying Egyptian pyramids (see Figure 6.7). Then, in supporting question three, students select from a list of other ancient societies (e.g., Mayans, Greeks, Aztecs, Indonesian) and investigate their pyramids.

FIGURE 6.7: A GUIDED INQUIRY BLUEPRINT ON PYRAMIDS

WHAT DO PYRAMIDS TELL US ABOUT THE PAST?

Kentucky Social Studies Standards	**2.20.** Students understand, analyze, and interpret historical events, conditions, trends, and issues to develop historical perspective. • Examine the rise of classical civilizations and empires (e.g., Greece and Rome) and analyze their lasting impacts on the world in the areas of government, philosophy, architecture, art, drama and literature
Staging the Compelling Question	Look at photographs of the excavation of the Pyramids of Giza and use the Question Formulation Technique (QFT) to generate questions about the Egyptian pyramids.

Supporting Question 1	Supporting Question 2	Supporting Question 3
	Guided Student Research	Independent Student Research
Where were the Egyptian pyramids?	What do the pyramids tell us about Egyptian society?	What do pyramids tell us about other ancient societies?
Formative Performance Task	Formative Performance Task	Formative Performance Task
List key features from a series of maps and describe how each map uniquely answers the question, "Where were the Egyptian pyramids?"	Write a description of each artifact and what it tells you about Egyptian society.	Research 3-5 artifacts found at other pyramids. Write a description of each artifact and what it tells you about the ancient society.
Featured Sources	Featured Sources	Featured Sources
Image bank of maps and images that show the location and features of Egyptian pyramids	Source packet: Artifacts that depict information about Egyptian governance, social classes, writing, technologies, religion	Select three to five sources to support research

Summative Performance Task	**ARGUMENT** *What do pyramids tell us about the past?* Construct an argument (e.g., detailed outline, poster, essay) that discusses the compelling question using specific claims and relevant evidence from historical sources.
	EXTENSION Create a museum exhibit that includes a replica of the pyramid studied along with five exhibition cards for artifacts that were found in or around the pyramid.
Taking Informed Action	**UNDERSTAND** Investigate the ethical, environmental, and/or historical challenges that modern-day archaeologists face as they unearth pyramids.
	ASSESS List the opportunities and challenges of uncovering the remains of lost societies.
	ACT Write an editorial for *Dig Into History* magazine that makes young readers aware of one or more problems archaeologists face in digging up the past.

CREATE INSTRUCTIONAL SCAFFOLDS TO STRUCTURE STUDENTS' RESEARCH. Because most students are novices when it comes to research, we suggest that teachers take the time to develop graphic organizers and other types of instructional scaffolds to prompt, structure, and guide student research. For example, in the elementary-level child activism inquiry, we created a three-column graphic organizer that included the activists' motivations, actions, and challenges faced. (See Figure 6.4 on page 109)

In the high school civil rights inquiry, teachers could create a similar graphic organizer that focuses on the historical actor, her actions, her impact, and the evidence that supports these elements. We provide the following descriptions of each element:

- Actor: An individual or organization that practiced nonviolent direct action during the Civil Rights Movement

- Actions: The contributions this individual or organization made to the particular event

- Impact: A claim about the individual or organization's impact on the event or movement

- Evidence: Specific evidence from sources (e.g., featured sources, textbooks, and website information) that describes the action this individual or organization took or its impact

Figure 6.8 represents a table useful to help to keep students focused around those key elements.

FIGURE 6.8: AN INSTRUCTIONAL SCAFFOLD FOR THE CIVIL RIGHTS INQUIRY

WHAT MADE THE _____ EFFECTIVE?			
Actors	Actions	Impact	Evidence

Teachers may want to further scaffold this work by providing an exemplar for students to follow. There is no "gotcha" in research. We want to set students up to be as successful as possible in their research endeavor. In the civil rights inquiry, teachers could provide students with this filled out example (see Figure 6.9) so they know exactly what we are hoping their research might include.

FIGURE 6.9: A SAMPLE ANSWER FOR THE GRAPHIC ORGANIZER IN THE CIVIL RIGHTS INQUIRY

WHAT MADE THE MONTGOMERY BUS BOYCOTT EFFECTIVE? (Teacher's guide to possible student responses)			
Actor(s)	Actions	Impact	Evidence
Rosa Parks	Refused to give up her seat to a white person on a bus in Montgomery, Alabama. Through her nonviolent actions and arrest, she inspired the boycott of the city buses.	Rosa Parks helped to end legal segregation by intentionally not giving up her seat on the bus and getting arrested. Additionally, her vocal support of the Montgomery Improvement Association throughout the boycott helped raise funding and awareness of the campaign.	Quote from Rosa Parks' autobiography: "I had no idea when I refused to give up my seat on that Montgomery bus that my small action would help put an end to the segregation laws in the South." Encyclopedia entry on Parks: "Parks inspired tens of thousands of black citizens to boycott the Montgomery city buses for over a year. During that period she served as a dispatcher to coordinate rides for protesters and was indicted, along with King and over 80 others, for participation in the boycott. Parks also made appearances in churches and other organizations, including some in the North, to raise funds and publicize the Montgomery Improvement Association (MIA)."

USE GUIDED INQUIRY WHEN YOU WANT TO COVER MULTIPLE EXAMPLES OF A TOPIC. One advantage of guided inquiry is that this blueprint structure allows teachers to cover more content ground. For example, in each of the inquiries featured above, the designer selected a slice of content to model for the whole class before expanding the content to include other people, events, and examples. In the elementary inquiry on child activism, students look closely at Malala before selecting from a list of 50 children who changed the world. In the middle grades inquiry on ancient pyramids, students take a deep dive into the Egyptian pyramids before selecting from a list of 10 other civilizations that erected pyramids. Lastly, in the high school civil rights inquiry, students examine the Greensboro Sit Ins along with a range of actors and non-violent actions that made history within the Civil Rights Movement.

Teachers using inquiry-based practices know all too well that content depth wins over content breadth the majority of the time. One advantage of a guided inquiry is that it can be structured so that students uncover more examples of a phenomenon and thus provide a more robust exploration into the broad ideas of social studies.

Affordances and Constraints of a Guided Inquiry

Expanding an inquiry so that students have an opportunity to be more independent in the research process is a worthwhile endeavor. Each blueprint featured in this book presents a unique set of instructional opportunities and challenges. The guided inquiry blueprint is no different. New experiences are afforded to students within a guided inquiry that allow students to practice selecting and vetting sources used within an inquiry.

In the table below, we summarize the instructional affordances and constraints of a Guided Inquiry.

TABLE 6.2: INSTRUCTIONAL AFFORDANCES AND CONSTRAINTS OF A GUIDED INQUIRY

GUIDED INQUIRY	
Instructional Affordances	Instructional Constraints
Gives students agency in the inquiry process	Takes more instructional time
Allows for research skill development	Necessitates access to a computer lab or media center
Provides students an opportunity to authentically use technology to find sources	Demands the teaching of research skills
Allows teachers to cover more examples of a topic or phenomenon	

Conclusion

In the next chapter, we further reimagine the blueprint so that students use it as a scaffold in conducting their own research. This fourth category of blueprint has been inspired by the IDM frontier teachers who have experimented with what we now call Student-Directed blueprints.

Appendix A

As part of the New York Toolkit Project (https://www.engageny.org/resource/new-york-state-k-12-social-studies-resource-toolkit), inquiry writers developed a set of 12 annotated inquiries, one per grade level that articulates both the curricular and instructional scaffolds that could be included in an inquiry. The table on the next page lists these annotated inquiries:

GRADE LEVEL	TOPIC	LINK
Kindergarten	Needs and Wants	http://www.c3teachers.org/inquiries/needsandwants/
1st Grade	Global Citizen	http://www.c3teachers.org/inquiries/globalcitizen/
2nd Grade	Civic Ideals	http://www.c3teachers.org/inquiries/civicideals-and-practices/
3rd Grade	Children's Rights	http://www.c3teachers.org/inquiries/childrens-rights/
4th Grade	New York Geography	http://www.c3teachers.org/inquiries/newyorkgeography/
5th Grade	Declaration of Independence	http://www.c3teachers.org/inquiries/declaration-of-independence/
6th Grade	Agriculture	http://www.c3teachers.org/inquiries/agriculture/
7th Grade	Uncle Tom's Cabin	http://www.c3teachers.org/inquiries/utc/
8th Grade	Japanese American Internment	http://www.c3teachers.org/inquiries/internment/
9th Grade	Aztecs	http://www.c3teachers.org/inquiries/aztec/
10th Grade	French Revolution	http://www.c3teachers.org/inquiries/frenchrev/
11th Grade	Civil Rights	http://www.c3teachers.org/inquiries/civil-rights/
12th Grade	Affordable Care Act	http://www.c3teachers.org/inquiries/affordable-care-act/

NOTES

1. R. K. Sawyer, *The Cambridge Handbook of the Learning Sciences* (New York: Cambridge University Press, 2006).

2. J. Saye and T. Brush, "Scaffolding Critical Reasoning about History and Social Issues in Multimedia-Supported Learning Environments," *Educational Technology Research and Development* 50 (2002), 77-96. Available online at: http://dx.doi.org/10.1007/BF02505026

3. D. Holton and D. Clark, "Scaffolding and Metacognition," *International Journal of Mathematical Education in Science and Technology* 37 (2006), 127–143.

4. J. Lee, S. G. Grant and K. Swan, in progress.

5. A. Weintraub and L. Horton, *Never Too Young!: 50 Unstoppable Kids Who Made a Difference* (New York: Sterling Children's Books, 2018).

6. *Ibid.*

7. *Ibid.*

8. K. Swan, J. Lee and S.G. Grant, *Inquiry Design Model: Building Inquiries in Social Studies* (Silver Spring, MD: National Council for the Social Studies and C3 Teachers, 2018).

CHAPTER 7

Student-Directed Inquiry: Handing the Blueprint Over to Students

Our aim in writing the *College, Career, and Civic Life (C3) Framework for State Social Studies Standards* was to change the tenor of state social studies standards from a patchwork of people, places, events, and thematic strands to the process of disciplined inquiry. In the first few lines of the C3 Framework, we call out this vision:

> Now more than ever, students need the intellectual power to recognize societal problems; ask good questions and develop robust investigations into them; consider possible solutions and consequences; separate evidence-based claims from parochial opinions; and communicate and act upon what they learn.[1]

At its heart, the C3 Framework seeks to empower students to be active participants in the coursework that makes up the social studies.

From our vantage point at C3 Teachers, we work with social studies teachers across the country as they engage students in complex disciplinary source work like the kind featured in the *structured* inquiry, "Can words lead to war?" We hear from C3 Teachers that their students are buzzing from their deliberations as they did during the *guided* inquiry, "How do children make history?" And, students in C3 classrooms practice with expert disciplinary tools such as historical empathy to understand controversial historical figures as they did in the *focused* inquiry, "How should we remember Christopher Columbus?" In all its forms, IDM blueprints can inspire teachers to create learning experiences that empower even our youngest social studies students.

Although we see the Inquiry Design Model (IDM) as a curricular tool for teachers wanting to engage students in disciplined inquiry, we always knew that teachers would need the curricular space to enable their students to ask their *own* questions; In the C3 Framework, we argue that students should develop "good questions and develop robust investigations into them."[2] In the first four types of blueprints presented in this book (e.g., structured, embedded, focused, and guided), teachers are in the driver's seat developing most, if not all, of the inquiry experiences for students. In this chapter, we present the *student-directed* blueprint, which provides a structure for students' autonomous research into the questions, tasks, and sources that make up any inquiry.

Up front, we want to acknowledge the ambitious C3 teachers who inspired the student-directed blueprint and helped kick its tires. This was not our innovation, but theirs. It was their belief in students' abilities and their desire for student agency within the inquiry experience that made us take a step back and expand our own thinking about the possibilities of the blueprint. Although the notion of a student-directed inquiry was our greatest hope, we couldn't see how it might work with a blueprint. We do now, thanks to the many teachers who have written us and shared their powerful stories—some of which we share in the sections below.

In this chapter, we unpack student-directed inquiry, noting from the onset that this is frontier territory. We begin with an examination of student agency as a conceptual overlay for thinking about independent inquiry. The teachers who have explored student-directed inquiry share a similar trait—they believe that students can do the work of constructing a blueprint for an inquiry. From that starting place, we look at the design and instructional considerations when teachers support students in developing their own inquiries. We conclude the chapter by discussing the instructional affordances and constraints teachers and their students face when employing this type of inquiry experience.

What Do We Mean by Student Agency?

Education does not suffer from a lack of ideas about how students learn and how teachers should facilitate that learning. One idea gaining attention right now is *student agency*, also known as *learner agency*. The notion of student agency can be traced back to the learning theory of constructivism. Broadly speaking, constructivism posits that learners are active creators of knowledge and are thereby agents of their own learning.[3] In order to construct knowledge, students need to ask questions, explore, and assess what they know in collaborative settings. This knowledge is influenced by learners' past experiences and is assimilated into new understandings with the teacher as a more knowledgeable guide.

Growing out of the ideas that comprise constructivist theory, student or learner agency assumes that students have a prominent role in their own learning. Lingden and McDaniel suggest that the "most transformative learning experiences will be those that are directed by the learner's own endeavors and curiosities."[4] More recent concepts that embody student agency are personalized learning or learner-centered education. These ideas have become popular again due in part to the enthusiasm for educational technology to personalize learning or to "flip" the locus of instruction to students using technology tools (e.g., the iPad, Internet).

Essentially, learning environments that elevate student agency give students a measure of power to act or direct their own learning. This approach may mean that students choose what they study (e.g., climate change, population growth, or a constitutional crisis), how they engage in the learning process (e.g. analyzing existing sources, collecting new data), and/or how they demonstrate their understandings (e.g., a five-paragraph essay, a poster, a digital documentary).

It is important to note that inquiry-based practice, regardless of blueprint type, offers a high-agency learning environment for students. For example, even when teachers craft the compelling question, they must represent student interest or relevance within a question. In doing so, they are acknowledging students' agency in the inquiry. Additionally, in all IDM inquiries, students are actively constructing knowledge by doing the disciplinary thinking required by the formative work. And, ultimately, students have voice in the inquiry when they construct *their* arguments and choose an appropriate modality for taking informed action as a result of the inquiry.

With that said, student-directed inquiry aims for the highest of high-agency learning environments. In student-directed inquiry, teachers hand over construction of a blueprint to students so that they can craft their own compelling questions and plan inquiries that they may, in turn, teach others. We only had to talk to these teachers for a few minutes to understand that their belief in the students' abilities drove the creation of the student-directed blueprint innovation. In the words of one teacher, the student-directed blueprint is "proof that students are more than capable to construct an IDM."[5]

In the section that follows, we look closely at the unique characteristics of a student-directed inquiry and then unpack a student example from a high school social studies classroom. From there, we summarize design and implementation tips from other teachers who have used student-directed inquiry in their own classrooms.

Characteristics of a Student-Directed Inquiry

A student-directed inquiry is designed so that students become more independent in the research process by planning to teach others about an important inquiry topic. In these inquiries, students construct the compelling and supporting questions as well as the formative and summative performance tasks, all with support from their teacher. (See Table 7.1) With additional backing from their teachers, students locate disciplinary sources to help answer the supporting questions and to help others learn through the inquiry process.

It is worth noting that student-directed inquiry is not for the faint of heart. Handing over the blueprint reins to students likely means more instructional time (and maybe additional instructional headaches)! There is really no way around this. At a minimum, teachers report that these kinds of independent research experiences take two weeks, but could take longer, depending on students' facility with research and how extensive a teaching experience is planned with other students or peers. In the section that follows, we walk through a high school student-directed inquiry on social movements and highlight its key elements, noting where appropriate the differences between it and the focused, structured, and guided blueprints.

TABLE 7.1 ELEMENTS OF A STUDENT-DIRECTED INQUIRY

STUDENT-DIRECTED INQUIRY	
Description	The student develops a blueprint around a question of interest and plans the inquiry using the blueprint. Teachers may ask students to use the blueprint to teach others.
Role of Teacher and/or Student in Blueprint Development	The student creates the blueprint with teacher guidance and feedback.
Questions	The student crafts the compelling and supporting questions with guidance from the teacher.
Tasks	The student constructs formative and summative performance tasks with guidance from the teacher.
Sources	The student selects disciplinary sources with guidance from the teacher.
Instructional Time	1-2 weeks for blueprint development; more time if students teach it.

Anatomy of a Student-Directed Inquiry Blueprint: What Makes a Movement Successful?

Like the inquiry blueprints featured in previous chapters, the student-directed inquiry blueprint is a one-page visual representation of the questions, tasks, and sources that define an inquiry. There are compelling and supporting questions, formative and summative performance tasks, and selected disciplinary sources that aid students in answering the inquiry's questions. The featured inquiry for this chapter was developed by a high school student from Kentucky, Wesley Wei. (See Figure 7.1 on page 124.) In the sections that follow, we walk through the blueprint elements and the unique approach that Wesley took while developing it.

Instructional Context

It is important to note the context of this student-directed inquiry. Wesley was a high school student in a 12th grade Advanced Placement Government class in rural Kentucky. His teacher, Mr. Ryan New, reports that his students had worked through six IDM inquiries during the course of the year and that he was explicit about the components of the blueprint as he and his students moved through each inquiry. For example, he used the terms compelling and supporting questions openly and students knew when they were engaged in a formative or summative performance task. The blueprint was a curricular map for students, where terms like Staging the Compelling Question and Taking Informed Action were not unspoken or tacit goals, but were a shared set of compass points for moving through the inquiry.

Students in Mr. New's class were given options for their final research project for the course. Some students chose to write a research paper and others chose to develop a blueprint that could be used to teach other students about a topic: In other words, students could develop an IDM inquiry-based curriculum in lieu of a 25-page paper. Five students chose the IDM option; Wesley was one of them. Although he didn't teach the inquiry, he constructed the blueprint in the hope that teachers would. His inquiry is now published on C3 Teachers: http://www.c3teachers.org/wp-content/uploads/2015/10/Kentucky-12-movemment_successfull.pdf

Questions

Like other inquiry types, student-directed inquiry begins with a topic that is fashioned into a compelling question. It should be both interesting to the student crafting it and academically worthwhile.

FIGURE 7.1: A STUDENT-DIRECTED INQUIRY BLUEPRINT ON SOCIAL MOVEMENTS

WHAT MAKES A MOVEMENT SUCCESSFUL?

C3 Framework Indicator	**D2.Civ.5.9-12:** Evaluate citizens' and institutions' effectiveness in addressing social and political problems at the local, state, tribal, national, and/or international level.
Staging the Compelling Question	Read *Changing Attitudes on Same Sex Marriage, Gay Friends, and Family* and discuss the LGBTQ+ movement with respect to the government and its policies on the local, state, and national levels.

Supporting Question 1	Supporting Question 2	Supporting Question 3	Supporting Question 4
Understand	**Understand**	**Understand**	**Understand**
How is the LGBTQ+ movement's progress affected by the public's reaction?	How have government leaders and policies impacted the movement?	How have the Supreme Court and precedence influenced the movement?	What role do people within the LGBTQ+ community play in the movement?
Formative Performance Task	**Formative Performance Task**	**Formative Performance Task**	**Formative Performance Task**
Fill out the Movement Analysis Organization Chart, analyzing the effect of the public reaction on the LGBTQ+ movement.	Add to the Movement Analysis Organization Chart, incorporating how the impacts of legislation and governmental figures affect the LGBTQ+ movement.	Add to the Movement Analysis Organization Chart, evaluating the decisions of the Supreme Court and its established precedence surrounding the LGBTQ+ movement.	Develop a claim that addresses how the movement was affected by the personal experiences of people within the LGBTQ+ community.
Featured Sources	**Featured Sources**	**Featured Sources**	**Featured Sources**
Source A: Compton's Cafeteria clips and article, *Screaming Queens*, NPR	**Source A:** "Hope Speech," Harvey Milk	**Source A:** *Romer v. Evans* Majority Opinion	**Source A:** "Coming Out To My Father," *The New Yorker*, Richard Socarides
Source B: "ERA and Homosexual 'Marriages'," *The Phyllis Schlafly Report*	**Source B:** Excerpts of various legislation impacting LGBTQ+ communities	**Source B:** *Lawrence v. Texas* Applicant Oral Argument and Dissenting Opinion	**Source B:** Images about the AIDS crisis
Source C: "From Montgomery to Stonewall" speech, Bayard Rustin	**Source C:** "Playing Politics at the Military's Expense," *The New York Times*	**Source C:** *United States v. Windsor* Majority Opinion	**Source C:** *The Politics of Being Queer*, Paul Goodman
Source D: "The Earth is Round," *It's Time*	**Source D:** "The Prime Rib of America," Lady Gaga	**Source D:** *Obergefell v. Hodges* Majority and Dissenting Opinions	**Source D:** *When We Rise*, Cleve Jones

Summative Performance Task	**ARGUMENT** What makes a movement successful? Construct an argument (i.e. essay or presentation) that addresses the compelling question, using specific claims and relevant evidence from historical and contemporary sources while acknowledging competing views.
	EXTENSION Participate in a Socratic Seminar about the LGBTQ+ community and movement, incorporating your personal experiences and perspective (e.g. from conversations, media, television/movies, etc.).
Taking Informed Action	**ASSESS** Research and discuss the current progress of the movement (i.e. rights given to members of the LGBTQ+ community) at the local, state, or national levels, considering it within the context of the larger movement.
	ACT Write to an outside institution (e.g. local newspaper, State Fairness Campaign, ACLU, etc.) discussing current policies and further steps needed.

Is the compelling question "What makes a movement successful?" relevant for students? Because Wesley crafted the question, it should be inherently interesting to students. Wesley shared the following note about what made the question relevant to him in a blog post on C3 Teachers:[6]

> With my teacher's help, I eventually leaned towards a subject which I was passionate about and believed could be thought-provoking, challenging, and compelling—the LGBTQ+ community and its movement. Quite frankly, this controversial subject was readily avoided in most classes, prompting me further to look into the subject.

"A subject which I was passionate about..." is music to any educator's ears. Wesley's passion for the subject fits half the criteria of the compelling question—it needs to be interesting to the student. Student-directed inquiry can super charge a compelling question by making it especially relevant.

One point to note is that student-directed compelling questions are not crafted completely independently. Wesley's teacher, Mr. New, played a critical role in helping shape the question from a topic Wesley was passionate about a question that could frame his investigation. Although students can identify issues, people, and events that they care about, they may be novices at channeling those interests into a functional, academically rigorous question.

Mr. New helped Wesley see the importance of the movement part of the LGBTQ+ movement. He talked with Wesley about historical parallels that could be drawn to other social movements, including the civil rights and women's suffrage movements. In doing so, Wesley was able to situate his question so that it addresses the enduring nature of any social movement. Crafting significant inquiry questions can be difficult for experienced teachers. Not surprisingly, students need models of compelling questions and guidance from their teachers to get to the just-right academic rigor of a compelling question.

According to Wesley, "the compelling question facilitated a structure where clear categories became evident." Again, with the help of his teacher, Wesley predicted a set of ideas that he would need to investigate in order to understand whether the LGBTQ+ movement was successful. He understood that he needed to know about the origins of the movement, how the public has reacted to it, the public policies that have shaped it, and the personal accounts of those influenced by it. As a result, Wesley created four supporting questions (SQs) that would serve as a useful structure for exploring these main ideas:

SQ1: How is the LGBTQ+ movement's progress affected by the public's reaction?

SQ2: How have government leaders and policies impacted the movement?

SQ3: How have the Supreme Court and precedence influenced the movement?

SQ4: What role do people within the LGBTQ+ community play in the movement?

Taken together, the four supporting questions offer a logical progression for understanding the growth of and resistance to the LGBTQ+ movement and the way in which it has changed over time. Using the compelling and supporting question architecture, Wesley was able to build out the formative and summative tasks and to locate disciplinary sources to help complete his investigation.

Tasks

As with all IDM inquiries, a student-directed inquiry is designed so that students answer the compelling question in the form of a summative argument. The formative performance tasks allow students a space to build up their content knowledge and to practice building an evidence-based argument.

Wesley's class had experience with constructing arguments within IDM inquiry. According to Mr. New, the students completed a total of six structured and focused IDM inquiries by the time Wesley tackled his blueprint in the late spring. As such, Wesley was familiar with claims, counter-claims, and how to use evidence from sources to support both. He understood that the compelling question set up the argumentative task. As part of the summative argument task development work, he crafted three argument stems to ensure his inquiry would enable students to answer the compelling questions from a variety of perspectives:

- A movement's success, such as the LGBTQ+ movement, is defined by its ability to sway public interest in its favor and to garner progressive action by government institutions like the Supreme

Court, advancing civil rights for the affected community in spite of setbacks dealt to the movement by the opposition.

- Though still ongoing, the LGBTQ+ movement demonstrates a successful movement as it is marked by changing government policies favorable to the LGBTQ+ community and a recent rise in conversation through "coming out" experiences, both of which were stimulated by activism by the public and members within the affected community.

- As a result of LGBTQ+ individuals vocalizing their deprivation of human rights and the public amplifying the same shortcomings, both groups were able to influence the policies and actions of the government, as well as Supreme Court decisions, all of which constitute essential aspects of a successful movement.

Wesley also valued the deliberative processes afforded by a Socratic discussion and so made it a part of his Summative Extension. And, because he wanted students to do something meaningful as a result of the investigation, Wesley sketched out a Taking Informed Action (TIA) sequence as a capstone for the inquiry. Knowing that his supporting questions would embed "understanding" into the formative work, he noted the following on his blueprint for the Assess and Act parts of the TIA sequence:

ASSESS: Research and discuss the current progress of the movement (i.e., rights given to members of the LGBTQ+ community) at the local, state, or national levels, considering it within the context of the larger movement.

ACT: Write to an outside institution (e.g., local newspaper, State Fairness Campaign, ACLU, etc.) discussing current policies and further steps needed.

Consistent with the IDM Design path, Wesley used the formative performance tasks to build up students' knowledge for the argument, Socratic discussion, and informed action sequence. Understanding how graphic organizers have helped him manage research and source work, Wesley created one to help students document their answers to the supporting questions. (See Figure 7.2 on page 128.) In doing so, he made filling out the graphic organizer a natural part of working through the four formative performance tasks.

WHAT MAKES A MOVEMENT SUCCESSFUL? Movement Analysis Organization Chart			
HOW DOES _____ AFFECT THE LGBTQ+ MOVEMENT?	ADVANCES What parts help accelerate the movement? Are the impacts short-felt or long-lasting?	INHIBITS Are there any aspects that slow down the progress of the movement? Have they dramatically impacted the movement, for better or worse?	TIMELINE AND SIGNIFICANCE How does the information correspond to the nature of the movement at the respective time (i.e., does it go with social understandings, or against?)
Supporting Question 1: Public Reaction			
Supporting Question 2: Government Leaders and Policies			
Supporting Question 3: Supreme Court and Precedence			
Supporting Question 4: People Within the LGBTQ+ Community *Develop a claim that addresses how the movement was uniquely affected by people within the LGBTQ+ community.*	CLAIM:		

The task of Staging the Compelling Question plays the role of peaking students' interest in an inquiry and enables them to begin playing with the big ideas embedded within the compelling question. The staging exercise sets the context for the inquiry. Wesley begins the inquiry with data from a survey by the Pew Research Institute in 2013[7] on the changing attitudes on same sex marriage, gay friends and family. (See Figure 7.3)

Wesley prompts teachers to use this source as the basis for an introductory discussion. Doing so sets the stage for the inquiry and introduces a set of ideas about what makes a movement successful.

Sources

Sources are the building blocks of an inquiry and allow students to acquire foundational knowledge about a topic and to understand the perspectives of those who either participated in an event or have thoughts about a topic under study. Wesley and his classmates

CHANGING ATTITUDES ON SAME-SEX MARRIAGE, GAY FRIENDS, AND FAMILY

MOST RESPONDENTS SEE THE LEGAL RECOGNITION OF SAME-SEX MARRIAGE AS "INEVITABLE"...

2013 **72**%

2004 **59**%

...EVEN OPPONENTS TO SAME-SEX MARRIAGE

AMONG THOSE WHO **FAVOR** SAME-SEX MARRIAGE — **85**% — THINK IT IS INEVITABLE

AMONG THOSE WHO **OPPOSE** SAME-SEX MARRIAGE — **59**% — THINK IT IS INEVITABLE

DO YOU PERSONALLY KNOW ANYONE WHO IS GAY OR LESBIAN?

2013 13% 87%

1993 38% 61%

HOW MANY PEOPLE WHO ARE GAY OR LESBIAN DO YOU KNOW?

A LOT **23**%   SOME **44**%

ONLY ONE OR TWO **19**%   NONE/ DON'T KNOW **13**%

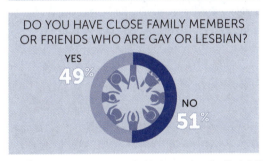

DO YOU HAVE CLOSE FAMILY MEMBERS OR FRIENDS WHO ARE GAY OR LESBIAN?

YES **49**%   NO **51**%

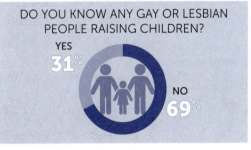

DO YOU KNOW ANY GAY OR LESBIAN PEOPLE RAISING CHILDREN?

YES **31**%   NO **69**%

Pew Research Center Survey on Same-Sex Marriage, conducted on May 1–5, 2013. Figures may not add to 100% because of rounding. "No" and "none" responses include those saying "don't know." 2004 survey conducted by the *Los Angeles Times*. 1993 survey conducted in June by NBC News/*Wall Street Journal*. The Pew Research Center survey is accessible at https://www.people-press.org/2013/06/06/in-gay-marriage-debate-both-supporters-and-opponents-see-legal-recognition-as-inevitable/

worked with sources over an entire year of academic study with Mr. New. Both teacher and student admitted that finding the right sources, and then editing and modifying them for other students, was by far the most challenging part of developing the inquiry. In his blog post, Wesley wrote, "hours spent digging through countless sources does a mind and body good!"[8] His commitment to good source work showed through in his blueprint.

In the IDM design process, we talk about a source logic needed when assembling sources for an inquiry.[9] As Wesley found out, teachers are faced with almost unlimited choices for both primary and secondary sources that can embellish and enliven an inquiry. A source logic helps teachers whittle down these sources to a collection that is manageable for students and offers an interesting texture to the sources they choose. Additionally, inquiry designers pay close attention to the role of sources in supporting arguments and must consider not only the relationship of the source to the supporting question, but also its use in completing the formative tasks and answering the compelling question. In other words, developing an inquiry's source logic can do a "mind and body good!"[10]

For the social movements inquiry, there is a strong source logic. First, the number of sources is manageable (four per supporting question) and they have been edited down within the body of the inquiry so that they can be accessed by most high school students. For example, in the opinions and dissenting opinions for featured sources used in Supporting Question 3, Wesley heavily excerpts the text into manageable chunks for students. The following excerpt was taken from the dissenting opinion of Supreme Court Justice Samuel Alito:[11]

> Today's decision... will be used to vilify Americans who are unwilling to assent to the new orthodoxy. In the course of its opinion, the majority compares traditional marriage laws to laws that denied equal treatment for African-Americans and women. The implications of this analogy will be exploited by those who are determined to stamp out every vestige of dissent.
>
> I assume that those who cling to old beliefs will be able to whisper their thoughts in the recesses of their homes, but if they repeat those views in public, they will risk being labeled as bigots and treated as such by governments, employers, and schools.... Recalling the harsh treatment of gays and lesbians in the past, some may think that turnabout is fair play. But if that sentiment prevails, the Nation will experience bitter and lasting wounds.

As we look across the featured sources in the formative work, we can also see an interesting source texture ranging from text-based to image-based sources. There are newspaper articles, speeches, Supreme Court decisions, videos, and photographs that help animate the inquiry and provide varying perspectives on the LQBTQ+ movement. From Lady Gaga and Harvey Milk to Phyllis Schlafly, Wesley tried to represent the many voices that contribute to our understanding of this important and controversial social movement. (See Figure 7.4)

FIGURE 7.4: FEATURED SOURCES FROM THE SOCIAL MOVEMENTS INQUIRY.

Featured Sources	Featured Sources	Featured Sources	Featured Sources
Source A: Compton's Cafeteria clips and article, *Screaming Queens*, NPR	**Source A:** "Hope Speech," Harvey Milk	**Source A:** *Romer v. Evans* Majority Opinion	**Source A:** "Coming Out To My Father," *The New Yorker*, Richard Socarides
Source B: "ERA and Homosexual 'Marriages'," *The Phyllis Schlafly Report*	**Source B:** Excerpts of various legislation impacting LGBTQ+ communities	**Source B:** *Lawrence v. Texas* Applicant Oral Argument and Dissenting Opinion	**Source B:** Images about the AIDS crisis
Source C: "From Montgomery to Stonewall" speech, Bayard Rustin	**Source C:** "Playing Politics at the Military's Expense," *The New York Times*	**Source C:** *United States v. Windsor* Majority Opinion	**Source C:** *The Politics of Being Queer*, Paul Goodman
Source D: "The Earth is Round," *It's Time*	**Source D:** "The Prime Rib of America," Lady Gaga	**Source D:** *Obergefell v. Hodges* Majority and Dissenting Opinions	**Source D:** *When We Rise*, Cleve Jones

In the previous chapter on guided inquiry, we said that teachers interested in that type of inquiry need to think about how students access sources (e.g., media center, in school, out of school). They also need to think about how to help their students assess the credibility of their found sources and to ensure that they find sources that represent a range of views. In the Design Considerations section that follows, we delve into some tips for helping students become better at making sure that the sources they locate can answer the compelling question, are credible, and provide a range of diverse perspectives.

Design Considerations for a Student-Directed Blueprint

When students build student-directed inquiries, they need guidance from their teachers. Teachers may want to introduce students to the 10-step IDM design process articulated in our last book, *Inquiry Design Model: Building Inquiries for the Social Studies Classroom.*[12] At the very least, it would be good to give them a primer on a "backward-design approach" to curriculum development. When we write curriculum, we start with the end in mind: students answer the compelling question in the form of an argument. Once those two points are established and understood, students can plan the best path to get to that argumentative destination using supporting questions, formative performance tasks, and sources as their stepping stones along that path.

In the following sections, we discuss additional design considerations when helping students construct a student-guided blueprint. These insights are a result of talking with a number of teachers who have innovated the blueprint to be an instructional research scaffold for students. To animate the points below, we continue to use the student-directed inquiry above (What makes a movement successful?) and add in two additional student-directed blueprints:

(1) "Should We Teach Evolution in Schools?" created by Chloe DeFrietas, a ninth grader from North Carolina; and (2) "Should Philosophy be a Mandatory Part of the Education System?" created by Morgan Seate, an eighth grader from North Carolina.

STUDENT-DIRECTED INQUIRY BEGINS WITH A BELIEF IN STUDENT AGENCY. One thing that teachers who do student-directed inquiry agree on is that students are capable of this kind of work. Mr. Ryan New said it this way:

> Wesley Wei's IDM about LGBTQ+ is proof that students are more than capable to construct an IDM blueprint. While I was there to help guide him through the structure of the blueprint, Wesley dove into questions, tasks, and sources, spending hours figuring out their connection. The result was incredible and is proof that often we need to trust our students and to mirror their energy and creativity.[13]

Russell McBride and Jeremy Thomas, social studies teachers in North Carolina, report that their belief in students' proficiency with student-directed inquiry led them to challenge one of their eighth-grade students to build an inquiry that would be the centerpiece of an initial professional learning experience for their colleagues. Morgan Seate, student inquiry developer, created the following inquiry around the compelling question "Should Philosophy be a Mandatory Part of the Education System?" (See Figure 7.5) Not only did Morgan design the inquiry, she also taught teachers in her school about the inquiry at the back-to-school event.

We continue to be inspired by our C3 teachers who do inquiry in the way that the rest of us breathe air. They just do not see any other way to teach but through inquiry.

STUDENT-DIRECTED INQUIRIES INCLUDE DIRECTION BY THE TEACHER, PARTICULARLY AROUND SOURCE WORK. All teachers we talked with agreed that the hardest part of the inquiry making process is the source work. This challenge is true when teachers create inquiries, and even truer when students create a student-directed inquiry. When we interviewed high school teacher Russell McBride and his colleague middle grades teacher Jeremy Thomas, they said that teaching their students about the nature and credibility of sources starts on day one of their classes. These teachers use a variety of tools to help students evaluate sources, but one design tip we share here is helping students evaluate their sources using the framework called a "Media Bias Chart," constructed by Ad Fontes Media in 2018.[14] (See Figure 7.6 on page 134.)

FIGURE 7.5: A STUDENT-DIRECTED INQUIRY BLUEPRINT ON CURRICULUM IN SCHOOLS

SHOULD PHILOSOPHY BE A MANDATORY PART OF THE EDUCATION SYSTEM?

Inquiry Standard	**12. C.1.1** Compare the various ways in which pragmatic and idealistic philosophies have addressed humanity's desire to understand life and the process of living.
Staging the Compelling Question	Have participants construct a list of the knowledge they have regarding the study of philosophy and then allow them to present their ideas with the rest of the class. After this is completed, have them watch a short video explaining what philosophy is in the sense of an academic discipline.

Supporting Question 1	Supporting Question 2	Supporting Question 3
What is the purpose of philosophy?	How is philosophy relevant to education?	What are the risks of teaching philosophy in schools?
Formative Performance Task	**Formative Performance Task**	**Formative Performance Task**
Have participants create a cartoon or picture depicting the purpose of philosophy.	Have participants write one to two paragraphs on the ways in which philosophy is relevant to education.	Have participants make their own advertisement explaining the risks of teaching philosophy in schools.
Featured Sources	**Featured Sources**	**Featured Sources**
Source A: Role of a Philosopher **Source B:** What's the Point of Philosophy? **Source C:** What is Philosophy for?	**Source A:** Why PLATO? **Source B:** Philosophy for Kids TED Talk **Source C:** BBC News Video	**Source A:** Let's Stop Trying to Teach Students Critical Thinking **Source B:** Philosophy and Depression **Source C:** Can Critical Thinking be Too Critical? **Source D:** The Philosopher's Problem

Summative Performance Task	**ARGUMENT** Should philosophy be a mandatory part of the education system? Construct an argument (e.g., detailed outline, poster, essay) that addresses the compelling question using specific claims and relevant evidence from historical and contemporary sources while acknowledging competing views.
	EXTENSION Have a class debate on whether or not philosophy should be a mandatory part of the education system.
Taking Informed Action	**UNDERSTAND** Have participants who feel philosophy should be a mandatory part of the education system create a lesson plan based on philosophy while those who do not believe in the teaching of philosophy do research on their own to find reasons other than the ones provided in the sources.
	ASSESS Have those who created a lesson plan teach a class of students using philosophy-based learning while those who did their own research compose a slideshow and present it to the class.
	ACT Have all participants write an email to their school board association addressing their point of view on philosophy being a mandatory part of the education system. Those who support philosophy would use the classes they taught to answer the compelling question in the affirmative, while those who were against philosophy being implemented would use the slideshow they created to compose their email.

FIGURE 7.6: MEDIA BIAS CHART

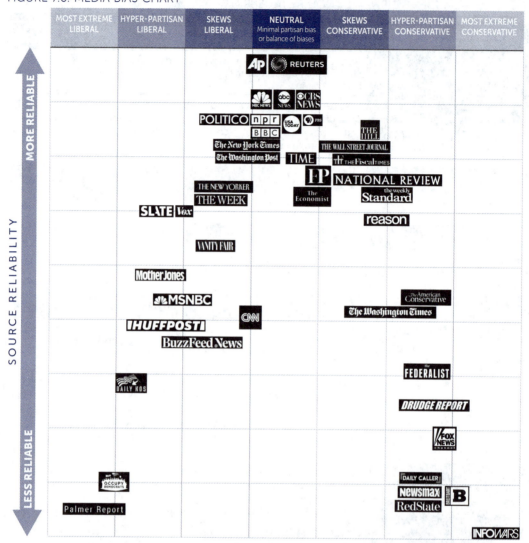

This chart, which constructs a framework for evaluating media sources, is derived from a media bias chart by Ad Fontes Media and represents the judgment of analysts using Ad Fontes Media's ranking methods in the time period for which the media sources were evaluated. More details about the methodology used to construct the media bias chart of Ad Fontes Media, as well as the range of coverage and interpretations offered by the media sources, are available at http://www.adfontesmedia.com.

Students developing their own inquiry are not necessarily asked to shy away from sources that have a partisan or extreme position, but they need to know why they are using those sources and to make sure to balance sources with multiple perspectives and strategies for students to recognize bias.

STUDENT-DIRECTED INQUIRY SHOULD NOT BE THE FIRST INQUIRY STUDENTS ENCOUNTER. Students who have engaged in this inquiry design have learned through inquiries previously. They bring a vernacular and lots of prior experience with compelling and supporting questions, with formative and summative performance tasks, and with primary and secondary sources. The teachers who do student-directed inquiry said their students use the blueprint to determine where they are in the investigation. This familiarity with the terms and flow of the instruction allowed the teachers to teach the instructional pedagogy more intuitively.

STUDENT-DIRECTED INQUIRY COULD RESULT IN STUDENTS TEACHING OTHER STUDENTS. Although Wesley Wei never taught his inquiry, other students have taught theirs. For example, Mr. Russell's ninth graders had taken Mr. McBride's inquiry class the previous year in eighth grade. These experienced inquiry learners developed and taught an inquiry as an assignment in Mr. Russell's ninth grade inquiry class. In the following inquiry, with the compelling question "Should Evolution Be Taught in Schools?" ninth grade social studies student Chloe DeFrietas developed an inquiry to teach middle school science students about the benefits and challenges of teaching evolution in science class. (See Figure 7.7 on page 136.)

All of the teachers who do student-directed inquiry asserted that the learning processes involved in teaching someone else are worth the extra effort. This only makes sense. Most of us became better students as a result of teaching. Teaching makes us become experts about the content we are teaching and inquiry-based curriculum forces us to push our thinking to the "so what?" of any topic.

Affordances and Constraints of a Student-Directed Inquiry

Providing students an opportunity to be more independent in the inquiry process is a worthwhile endeavor. Each blueprint presented in this book offers a unique set of instructional opportunities and challenges. The student-directed inquiry blueprint is no different. In the table below, we summarize the instructional affordances and constraints of a Student-Directed Inquiry.

TABLE 7.2: INSTRUCTIONAL AFFORDANCES AND CONSTRAINTS OF A STUDENT-DIRECTED INQUIRY

STUDENT-DIRECTED INQUIRY	
Instructional Affordances	Instructional Constraints
Enables high levels of learner agency in the inquiry process; students are extremely proud of the results.	Takes more instructional time
Allows for extensive inquiry skill development.	Demands that students have a lot of practice with other kinds of blueprints before tackling a student-directed blueprint.
Helps teachers connect students with what they are passionate about.	Necessitates teaching curriculum development skills
Makes students feel like experts, reporting they feel like they are in college.	Requires teaching the curricular vocabulary (e.g., formative performance task) of the blueprint
	Can be too challenging for younger students.

SHOULD EVOLUTION BE TAUGHT IN SCHOOLS?

Inquiry Standard	**Bio.3.4** Explain the theory of evolution by natural selection as a mechanism for how species change over time.
Staging the Compelling Question	Watch a crash course video that explains the history of evolution and then discuss the reactions that occurred during that time in response to this new found theory and compare them to the current day.

Supporting Question 1	Supporting Question 2	Supporting Question 3
What is evolution?	Why is teaching evolution beneficial?	How could teaching evolution be detrimental?
Formative Performance Task	**Formative Performance Task**	**Formative Performance Task**
Illustrate a comic strip that explains what evolution is and the evidence surrounding it.	Create a T-chart that explains the benefits of teaching evolution in the classroom.	Using the T-chart from SQ 2, explain the disadvantages of teaching evolution in the classroom.
Featured Sources	**Featured Sources**	**Featured Sources**
Source A: A Pew research timeline of evolution beginning with the life of Charles Darwin	**Source A:** A discussion on why evolution is a part of scientific standards	**Source A:** Opinion article on how evolution is harder to grasp for creationist students
Source B: A Smithsonian discussion of all the evidence found in favor of evolution	**Source B:** A brief discussion on why evolution should be taught as fact, not theory	**Source B:** Article on granting legal protection for teachers who teach creationism
Source C: A *Live Science* definition of evolution and the evidence behind it	**Source C:** *Newsweek* article on why evolution should be taught to children before high school	**Source C:** Statistics revealing the opinions of teachers on the subject of evolution vs. creationism

Summative Performance Task	**ARGUMENT** Should Evolution be Taught In Schools? Construct an argument (e.g., detailed outline, poster, essay) that addresses the compelling question using specific claims and relevant evidence from historical and contemporary sources while acknowledging competing views.
	EXTENSION Create a five minute podcast that argues whether or not evolution should be taught in schools and how it should be utilized. Use at least three outside sources to complete your argument and include specific details as well as a solution to the issue.
Taking Informed Action	**UNDERSTAND** Be able to fully understand and grasp the current-day debate on whether evolution has a place in the classroom.
	ASSESS Understand the differences of opinion in the U.S. on the issue and what the majority of public schools are currently teaching in regard to human evolution.
	ACT Construct a well-informed and formal letter to your principal that explains why you believe evolution should or should not have a place in the classroom; also, gather a portion of the student body's opinion on the subject.

In weighing the advantages and disadvantages of handing over the blueprint to students, it seems only fitting that we look to students for why this approach might be worth the effort. Wesley responded this way:

From both making *and* answering inquiries, I've witnessed my growth in skills, such as analyzing and evaluating evidence, drawing comparisons, synthesizing information, and creating logical arguments. Personally, in the process of creating this IDM, I was tasked with balancing my limited scope of knowledge with a new mode of presentation, uprooting the typical style of learning. It was a learning curve, but one that has a great potential to transform classrooms.

We do love our IDM learning curves along with all the other inspiring ideas that Wesley shares:

- Growth in skills

- Creating logical arguments

- Uprooting the traditional scope of knowledge

- Potential to transform classrooms.

Yes, please!

Conclusion

Where do we go from here? In the next chapter, we look at the ways that teachers have looped different inquiries across their curriculum to create horizontal alignment around inquiry. Then, we look at the ways departments, professional learning communities (PLCs), and districts have looped IDMs across grade levels to create vertical alignment around inquiry.

NOTES

1. National Council for the Social Studies (NCSS), *College, Career, and Civic Life (C3) Framework for Social Studies State Standards* (Silver Spring, MD: NCSS, 2013), 6.

2. *Ibid.*

3. J. S. Bruner, "The Act of Discovery," *Harvard Educational Review* 31 (1961), 21-32; J. Dewey, *The Quest for Certainty: A Study of the Relation of Knowledge and Action* (New York: Minton, Balch, 1929); J. Piaget, *The Origins of Intelligence in Children* (New York: International Universities Press, 1952); L. S. Vygotsky, "Thought and Word," in L. Vygotsky E. Hanfmann, and G. Vakar (Eds.), *Studies in Communication. Thought and Language* (Cambridge, MA: MIT Press, 1962), 119-153.

4. R. Lingden and R. McDaniel, "Transforming Online Learning through Narrative and Student Agency," *Educational Technology and Society* 15, no. 4 (2012), 344-355 at page 346.

5. W. Wei, "Student blogger: What makes a movement successful?" [Blog Post, 2017], C3Teachers. Retrieved from: http://www.c3teachers.org/student-blogger-makes-movement-successful/

6. *Ibid.*

7. Pew Research Center, *Changing Attitudes on Same Sex Marriage, Gay Friends, and Family*, June 6, 2013. Accessed at http://pewrsr.ch/10T0s4N

8. W. Wei, *op. cit.*

9. K. Swan, J. Lee and S.G. Grant, *Inquiry Design Model: Building Inquiries in Social Studies* (Silver Spring, MD: National Council for the Social Studies and C3 Teachers, 2018).

10. W. Wei, *op. cit.*

11. See *Obergefell v. Hodges.* (n.d.). *Oyez.* Retrieved February 12, 2019, from https://www.oyez.org/cases/2014/14-556

12. K. Swan, J. Lee and S.G. Grant, *op. cit.*

13. W. Wei, *op. cit.*

14. See the "Media Bias Chart," Ad Fontes Media (2018), accessed at https://www.adfontesmedia.com

CHAPTER 8

Looping Inquiry

How do you build your house of inquiry? Which rooms will be the biggest? Smallest? What sequence of inquiries will you create to make your inquiry house feel like a home? These questions are at the heart of this book and central to this chapter. But, before we get there, let's do a quick recap.

So far, we have constructed an inquiry house with three major parts. First, there is the inquiry foundation that includes the essential elements to any inquiry—questions, tasks, and sources. Then, we presented five rooms in the house, each representing a different kind of inquiry (structured, embedded action, focused, guided, and student-directed). But we have yet to finish the house with a curriculum roof. A roof is constructed when teachers start to sequence blueprints in such a way that they become a curriculum and a coherent course of study in which teachers clarify the number and type of blueprints they intend to use and how they plan to space those blueprints across the school year. In making these decisions, a roof begins to emerge. The roof, or a teacher's approach to building an inquiry-based curriculum, ultimately completes the house of inquiry.

In this chapter, we discuss the process of curriculum roof building as it relates to inquiry generally and IDM specifically. The concept behind that activity is looping. The roof completes and integrates a house, and looping plays an essential role in the construction of a roof that can can hold the house together. We begin by taking a look at how some teachers have constructed their curricular roofs so that inquiry loops across a course of study. We refer to this approach as a *horizontal* loop. Next, we examine departmental and district examples of curricular looping where inquiry is developed across grade levels. We refer to this approach as a *vertical* loop. We end the chapter with design considerations for blueprinting inquiry across the curriculum and the affordances and constraints of approaching inquiry-based curriculum this way.

What Do We Mean by Looping Inquiry?

Ideally, inquiry is not a once-in-a-while experience. After all, inquiry is the essence of social studies[1] and we know students need lots and lots of practice to get better at it. In other words, we want inquiry to *loop* throughout the social studies curricula. What do we mean by the term "looping"? At its simplest, we mean offering students opportunities to engage in inquiry in regular intervals and in a coherent fashion within and across grade levels.[2]

In a discussion of how curricular depth can be attained through looping, Walter Parker has pointed out that "deeper learning requires…a kind of instruction that affords iteration of core concepts and skills. This means revisiting them periodically in different contexts. This quasi-repetitive cycling results in knowing them in a more complex and adaptive way. This is deeper learning." He points out that looping, or spiral curriculum development across grade levels, "has an honored place in the social studies," but it can also be "done across units within a single course." This kind of spiral instruction "allows the core concepts and skills to be applied in different scenarios. This adds complexity, thanks to the novelty of each context … and it affords adaptivity."[3]

In this chapter, we refer to looping across a course of study as horizontal looping, and to departmental and district examples of curricular looping where inquiry is developed across grade levels as vertical looping. We will present examples of horizontal looping that develops the abilities of students to investigate multiple perspectives, and to investigate social issues using skills acquired from different social studies disciplines. We will also offer an example of how looping across grade levels (vertical looping) offers teachers valuable opportunities to build up the inquiry-based skills of their students over time by developing a pacing guide that maps out the scope and sequence of important social studies content.

Looping is not a new idea. Almost sixty years ago, Jerome Bruner wrote, "we begin with the hypothesis that any subject can be taught in some intellectually honest form to any child at any stage of development."[4] In other words, even the most complex social studies ideas, if properly structured and presented, can be understood by very young children. Looping or spiraling curriculum is an outgrowth of this foundational belief. Like Bruner, we believe that novices can engage with really complex ideas (e.g., human rights, spatial reasoning, economic decision making) using challenging inquiry skills (e.g., questioning, source work, argumentation). And they can do this work if the ideas and processes are thoughtfully staged so that students encounter them first in their simplest forms and then move to more sophisticated forms. Each time students revisit the idea and/or process, it is reinforced and solidified until they begin to demonstrate some degree of facility with the ideas and with the skills.

In the following three sections, we look at looping IDM inquiries. We begin with an eleventh-grade teacher from Kentucky who horizontally loops inquiry across a U.S. History course using a series of focused inquiries. Then, we examine a third-grade curriculum designed by a team of teachers in New York who use a variety of inquiry types to animate three major concept anchors in their curriculum. Finally, we highlight a vertically looped inquiry-based curriculum crafted by a team of middle school teachers from Illinois.

Looping Focused Inquiries Across a Course: An Eleventh-Grade Example

Let's think about curricular looping through the lens of one high school teacher, Mr. Ryan Lewis. Mr. Lewis feels that his students benefit from seeing history and the world through multiple perspectives. He understands that we live in a pluralist democracy, that perspective-taking is a critical civic skill, and that history provides the subject matter to exercise this important disciplinary practice. He uses the following history indicator from the C3 Framework to guide the inquiries in his curriculum: D2.His.4.9-12.[5] Analyze complex and interacting factors that influenced the perspectives of people during different historical eras.

Early in the school year, Mr. Lewis realizes that this is the first time that his students have studied history in this way or seen events or people from multiple points of view. So he launches his U.S. history class with a short exercise in which students examine multiple perspectives on Christopher Columbus by viewing two different images of him. (See Figure 8.1 on page 142) This was an exercise that was also featured in Chapter 5 in a middle school inquiry.

Students practice comparing and contrasting the two images and thinking about how their textbook portrays this controversial but historically significant figure. Students struggle a bit in analyzing the images (e.g., breaking down the image, understanding artistic elements that convey perspective), but they enjoy questioning the sources and building their own historical interpretations of Columbus.

FIGURE 8.1: TWO ARTISTS' RENDERINGS OF CHRISTOPHER COLUMBUS

Engraving by Theodor de Bry depicting the controversial account by Bartolomé de las Casas regarding the *Brevísima relación de la destrucción de las Indias* (A Short Account of the Destruction of the Indies), 1552.

Painting by John Vanderlyn depicting Columbus claiming possession of the New World in caravels, the Niña and the Pinta. *Landing of Columbus* (1842–47), U.S. Capitol Rotunda, Washington, D.C.

Mr. Lewis knows that he has to repeat this process again with his students to help them improve their perspective-taking skills and to have this skill stick. When the class begins to study the founding period of the United States, he asks students to examine Thomas Jefferson in the same way that they approached Columbus. This time, he expands the source set to include three primary sources including text-based sources that portray conflicting perspectives of this similarly flawed but key historical figure. He asks the students to compare and contrast these perspectives and to craft a complex depiction of the third President. Students are less tentative this time around as they make connections to the Columbus exercise they completed a month earlier.

But, Mr. Lewis is not finished with multiple perspectives. Moreover, he wants to deepen his students' examinations by expanding the exercise with different historical actors, more sophisticated source sets, and more thorough and complete claim-making exercises. So, he designs additional inquiries with other historical actors they encounter over the year (e.g., Andrew Jackson, Nat Turner, John Brown, Elizabeth Cady Stanton), adding additional sources and secondary scholarship and asking that students develop claims that are clearer and supported with multiple forms of evidence. By the end of the year, students are more comfortable interrogating sources and reconciling multiple perspectives represented in these sources to understand the country's past and people.

FIGURE 8.2: A HORIZONTAL CURRICULUM LOOP FEATURING HISTORICAL ACTORS

INQUIRY 1 · INQUIRY 2 · INQUIRY 3 · INQUIRY 4 · INQUIRY 5 · INQUIRY 6

MULTIPLE PERSPECTIVES

FALL · WINTER · SPRING

In these ways, Mr. Lewis excels in the art of looping inquiry. He intentionally structures a series of inquiry-based experiences so that they both recur and ratchet up over the course of the year. Using a series of focused IDM blueprints, he consistently emphasizes the core skill of understanding why individuals and groups may have different perspectives. But he does so by making the exercises students complete increasingly sophisticated and challenging. In this way, Mr. Lewis creates a *horizontal* loop across his curriculum. (See Figure 8.2)

Mr. Lewis has constructed his curricular home with questions, tasks, and sources as the foundation. He repeats the *question*, "How should we remember..." across the school year, inserting a chronological series of historical actors. The *tasks* he assigns ask students to answer these questions with arguments comprised of claims supported with evidence that they pull from the *sources* they encounter. He keeps the inquiries interesting by increasing the number and sophistication of the sources and by expecting that his students' responses to the argumentation tasks become more complex, clear, and coherent. And, he stays true to his disciplinary and civic aims of teaching students to consider multiple perspectives when viewing the past. The roof on the curricular house has been constructed as he articulates a coherent loop around inquiry.

FIGURE 8.3: CONSTRUCTING A CURRICULAR HOUSE

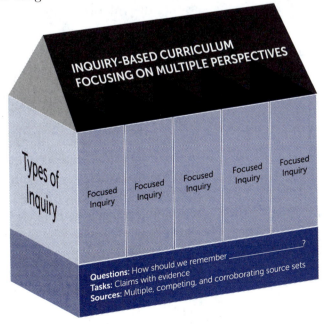

INQUIRY-BASED CURRICULUM FOCUSING ON MULTIPLE PERSPECTIVES

Types of Inquiry

Focused Inquiry | Focused Inquiry | Focused Inquiry | Focused Inquiry | Focused Inquiry

Questions: How should we remember _____?
Tasks: Claims with evidence
Sources: Multiple, competing, and corroborating source sets

Using focused inquiry blueprints across a course of study is an important step in making social studies courses truly inquiry-based. But Mr. Lewis's approach is simply one of many. In fact, teachers might decide to use all of the inquiry types (structured, embedded, focused, guided, and student-directed) within a course of study or choose to use only one, two, or three inquiry types. We illustrate one of these approaches in the next section.

Looping Different Kinds of Inquiry Across a Course: A Third-Grade Example

To build an inquiry-based curriculum, students need to engage in inquiry more than once. We do not want to prescribe how many inquiry experiences students should have in a year, but we know these experiences need to be regular. In the last section, we examined one way of creating a horizontal loop by using a series of focused inquiries within a course of study. But teachers needn't be confined to this approach.

A recent example of horizontal looping comes from a group of third-grade teachers in Syracuse, New York. In this district, social studies is taught in three eight-week units across the year. Each unit consists of 2-4 inquiries that explore a range of topics related to world geography, human rights, economics, and local government. (See Figure 8.4) The goal of the social studies curriculum is to have students investigate a range of social issues using disciplinary tools such as maps, data, and historical documents and to practice with inquiry skills regularly. The third-grade teachers want to empower their students to engage with these skills and take action using IDM as the curricular mechanism.

The blueprints the teachers developed loop four different types of inquiry (focused, structured, embedded action, and guided) throughout the units of study. Their main goal was to have students see social studies through compelling questions and to realize that answers to those questions require them to respond with evidence that supports a position. In other words, they wanted students to practice with the elements of questions, tasks, and sources of an IDM inquiry. While each inquiry has an action opportunity, the final inquiry for each unit was constructed to include a sequence for Taking Informed Action so that students could work outside the classroom on an issue that impacts their community.

Unit 1 of the third-grade curriculum is dedicated to topics within world geography. Students examine different kinds of maps (Inquiry 1), issues of water stress (Inquiry 2), and the disposal of garbage

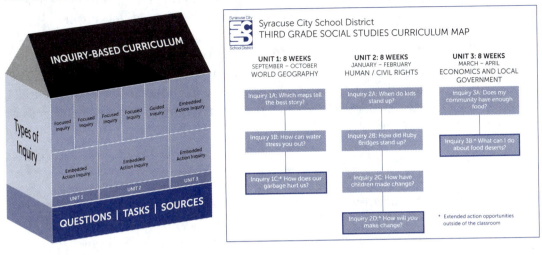

(Inquiry 3). The first two inquiries are focused inquiries; the third inquiry is an embedded action inquiry. The third inquiry uses a taking informed action sequence that highlights the issue of trash and its impact on the community. Students begin the sequence by conducting an audit of their school's waste. Then, students determine different ways that they could help the community reduce the amount of waste. Finally, the students propose a school-wide initiative to reduce the waste and work with the school's administration to raise awareness and to implement the solution.

In the second unit, students follow a similar inquiry pattern when looking at the broad issue of civil rights, except that there are four inquiries. They begin with two focused inquiries (When do kids stand up? and How did Ruby Bridges stand up?) where they examine historical examples of children engaging in non-violent protest during the 1960s. Then, they work through a guided-inquiry blueprint focusing on children from around the world who have made social change. In the "How will you make change?" embedded action inquiry, the taking informed action sequence asks students to examine an issue that is important to them, assess what can be done to help with the issue, and plan ways they can take action on their issue. Ultimately, teachers help students take action based on their research.

The final unit focuses on economics and local government. Here, students examine the urban problem of food deserts within an embedded action inquiry that features the compelling question, "Does my community have enough food?" Students then segue to a related inquiry with the compelling question, "What can I do about food deserts?" The taking informed action sequence enables students to work with local government officials to determine how they might raise awareness around this pervasive local issue.

Taken together, these third-grade teachers constructed a sophisticated curricular roof on their inquiry house. By focusing on questions, tasks, and sources and highlighting action as an essential civic skill, they have created a coherent curriculum with inquiry as its center.

Regardless of how a group of teachers decide to loop their inquiries or build their IDM house, one major advantage is the opportunity to help students build their content knowledge and skills over time. We know that inquiry is not a one-and-done kind of idea. Students need to learn how to wrestle with sources, develop and support claims and counter-claims, and construct and support arguments. Mastery of these skills takes time. Teachers who invest their curricular time in inquiry should expect to see a maturation in their students' use of concepts and skills over time, as well as their comfort in asking their own questions, and their reactions to the uncertainty of more than one valid answer.

The other big advantage of looping inquiries is the opportunity to build teachers' competence, confidence, and experience with inquiry. Curricular change always comes with apprehension. Any move toward an inquiry-based approach is likely to feel a little risky, so having the time to adjust is important, as is support from the school system. Building a community of like-minded supporters, including colleagues and administration, is key to lasting curricular change through inquiry.

In the next section, we examine how one group of middle-school educators created a series of interconnected horizontal curricular loops across different grade levels. In so doing, they introduced us to the idea of a vertical loop.

Looping Inquiry Across Grade Levels: A Middle School Example

The evidence is building—inquiry-based teaching and learning can produce some pretty amazing results.[6] The work that individual teachers do matters, but imagine how powerful it would be if inquiry became a way of school life for students from kindergarten on. School districts that decide to invest in inquiry as a K-12 experience offer their students a remarkable opportunity to build their social studies content knowledge and disciplinary skills. They also offer their teachers a valuable opportunity to build out their inquiry-based practices across time and with the support of their colleagues.

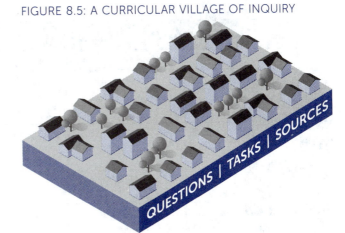

FIGURE 8.5: A CURRICULAR VILLAGE OF INQUIRY

QUESTIONS | TASKS | SOURCES

In the previous sections, we highlighted two examples of horizontal looping where inquiry was purposefully repeated across a course of study. But what happens when grade levels band together to make a single house of inquiry part of a larger village or community? (See Figure 8.5.) Recently, we worked with a group of middle school teachers in Northshore, Illinois who did just that. While wanting to remain in control of the day-to-day instruction, they collectively knew they wanted to do a better job keeping the same pace within grade levels and, more importantly, they wanted all students to experience IDM inquiry at least four times a year. Ultimately, the teachers hoped that they would see students' opportunities to learn with questions, tasks, and sources grow over time.

Teachers began by collaboratively developing a pacing guide that mapped out the scope and sequence of content in the sixth, seventh, and eighth grades. From there, they came to consensus on the topics they liked most and selected one topic for each grading period: early fall, late fall, winter, and spring. For example, in the seventh grade, which focuses on U.S. History from the founding period through the Civil War, the teachers chose to do inquiries on the Declaration of Independence, Hamilton versus Jefferson, the Louisiana Purchase, and slavery.

On reflection, it appears that these Illinois teachers engaged in a fairly simple task. It is not. It is hard to open up your curriculum for colleagues to examine and judge. Imagine the thought bubbles when one of the eighth-grade teachers said that he had barely reached the Cold War by the end of school while all of the other teachers were well into the Civil Rights movement of the 1960s. These are not easy conversations, especially when you have to agree on which topics are most suited for inquiry. However, these teachers knew that this kind of curricular articulation (and honesty) was needed if they were going accomplish their ambitious inquiry goals.

		FEATURED INQUIRIES			
		Early Fall	Late Fall	Winter	Spring
GRADE LEVEL	TIMING	1ST INQUIRY	2ND INQUIRY	3RD INQUIRY	4TH INQUIRY
6th Grade	Topic	Early Societies	Ancient Civilizations	Early Democracy	Project Citizen
	Compelling Question	Is growth always good?	What do the pyramids tell us about the past?	What is a vote worth?	How can I make change?
7th Grade	Topic	Colonial America	Constitution	Louisiana Purchase	Fugitive Slave Act
	Compelling Question	Why do countries declare independence?	Hamilton or Jefferson: With whom do you agree?	How free was the "Empire of Liberty?"	Did the Fugitive Slave Act weaken or strengthen slavery?
8th Grade	Topic	Industrial Revolution	1920s	Genocide	McCarthyism
	Compelling Question	How did the Industrial Revolution move people?	What made the 20s roar?	Are bystanders guilty too?	How do politicians use fear?

Once they established their pacing guides and generated a set of inquiry topics, the teachers began developing a series of blueprints that animated the topics. For example, in the eighth grade, teachers developed inquiries on the Industrial Revolution (How did the Industrial Revolution move people?), the 1920s (What made the 20s roar?), the Holocaust (Are bystanders guilty too?), and the Cold War (How do politicians use fear?). (See Figure 8.6)

After building their horizontal grade level loops, they worked as a middle school social studies department to think about students' experience with inquiry from sixth to eighth grade. One decision they made was to use more focused inquiries in the sixth grade and more structured inquiries in the eighth grade. Why? These teachers believed their students came into sixth grade social studies with very little experience with argumentation and source work. They believed that more sustained

FIGURE 8.7: A VERTICAL CURRICULUM LOOP

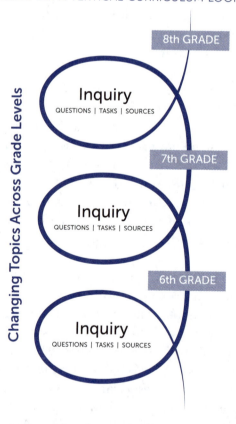

Changing Topics Across Grade Levels

8th GRADE

Inquiry
QUESTIONS | TASKS | SOURCES

7th GRADE

Inquiry
QUESTIONS | TASKS | SOURCES

6th GRADE

Inquiry
QUESTIONS | TASKS | SOURCES

forms of inquiry could increase with maturity and experience. As these teachers worked together across grade levels to create common inquiry experiences, they were creating a *vertical curricular loop*—a cohesive approach to inquiry within and across grade levels. (See Figure 8.7)

Design Considerations for Looping Inquiry

How should teachers, departments, and districts loop inquiry in their classrooms? We always come back to the craft of teaching and trusting that teachers know their own styles, what makes sense for their students, and how the content of the course is best animated by inquiry. Although we hope that readers are inspired by the curricular stories presented in this chapter, we think teachers should ultimately decide what kind of inquiry house they build. Those questions include how many rooms (or inquiries), what kinds of rooms (or inquiries), and what kind of roof (or curriculum) creates a coherent structure. With that said, we offer the following design guidance that we have learned from the many teachers who have inspired us in our IDM journey.

TEACHERS WANTING TO LOOP INQUIRY HORIZONTALLY OR VERTICALLY CAN FIND SOME HELP ON THE C3 TEACHERS WEBSITE. Inquiries on C3 Teachers are available in Word at www.c3teachers. org so that teachers across the country can make these inquiries right for their students. Whether that means changing up sources, adding a supporting question, or making the informed action opportunity more applicable to a particular group of students, teachers have the ability to abbreviate, modify, or extend a wide range of published inquiries. These inquiries are housed within a database that is searchable by grade level and topic. We encourage teachers to use existing inquiries in their curricular loops if it will save them time and provide some needed momentum in getting started on tackling the goal of an inquiry-based curriculum.

ANTICIPATE DISAGREEMENTS OVER CONTENT EMPHASIS. As we said above, looping asks educators to articulate their instructional goals in terms of content and skills and to discuss current instructional methods and resources. Examining current practices is likely to surface differences in approaches towards teaching social studies. The old adage, "don't take it personally," will not be helpful here. Teaching *is* personal. It is a craft that is artfully expressed by an individual teacher. As teachers engage in curricular conversations, we think it needs to be done reverently. While inquiry is a powerful tool, it is not the only pedagogical tool, and we want to be careful not to trample over other instructional techniques. For example, if your colleagues are proud of their long-successful elementary "Colonial Christmas" experience, make inquiry loop around a different topic. No need to draw blood here. Teachers should be proud of the work they do and inquiry should empower, not undermine, ambitious teachers.

INQUIRY DEMANDS TRUST. Moving away from traditional practices can be risky for teachers and their students. Teachers may worry that their students won't be able or willing to rise to the increased academic challenge; students may worry that their teachers will judge their fledgling efforts too harshly. We think that these worries will begin to evaporate once teachers and students work through an inquiry. Still, it may take a while before either group is comfortable in an inquiry-rich environment.

Key to building that comfort is trust, and trust that flows in both directions. Teachers need to trust that their students will take a compelling question seriously, that they'll be willing to work through a range of sources, that they'll be able to construct evidence-based arguments, and that they'll propose taking informed action projects that won't get their teachers fired. For their part, students need to trust that their teachers will help them recognize the changes an inquiry-based approach demands, that they'll understand why students may struggle with the idea that there is not one right answer, that they'll encourage and support students through their fumbling and missteps, and that they won't give up on inquiry and their students if the initial effort does not go as planned.

Affordances and Constraints of Looping Inquiry

If creating one inquiry is hard, then making multiple inquiries is harder, and then getting one's colleagues on board is harder still. That said, we think the advantages of creating a cohesive inquiry-based curriculum far outweigh the challenges teachers are bound to face. In Table 8.1, we conclude by summarizing the affordances and constraints of looping inquiry.

TABLE 8.1: AFFORDANCES AND CONSTRAINTS OF LOOPING INQUIRY

LOOPING INQUIRY	
Affordances	Constraints
Builds students' inquiry skills over time.	Necessitates sometimes challenging discussions among teachers across grade levels.
Creates consistency and coherence of curriculum.	Requires consensus building and may require coordination (and persuasion) of grade-level colleagues to an inquiry-based approach.
Offers teachers opportunities to build their inquiry-based practices over time.	Requires careful and consistent pacing of content.
Offers teachers and administrators opportunities to see growth in students' knowledge and skills.	
Sets teachers up for meaningful assessment, grading, and reporting.	

Conclusion

Teaching through inquiry can free up our thinking about the content we teach, the instructional approaches we use, and the formative and summative assessments that we plan. Looping offers teachers ways to see, for example, how students are developing as argument makers over the course of their K-12 lives. Our hope is that teachers will realize that inquiry is a lifelong practice and one that is always under construction. In the next chapter, we build upon the curricular looping ideas and discuss how these moves toward curricular coherence can lead the way to meaningful assessment.

NOTES

1. National Council for the Social Studies (NCSS), *College, Career, and Civic Life (C3) Framework for Social Studies State Standards* (Silver Spring, MD: NCSS, 2013).

2. W. Parker, "Projects as the Spine of the Course: Design for Deeper Learning," *Social Education* 82, no. 1 (January-February 2018), 45–48.

3. *Op. cit.* at page 47.

4. J. Bruner, *The Process of Education* (New York: Vintage, 1960), 33.

5. *College, Career, and Civic Life (C3) Framework for Social Studies State Standards* at page 47.

6. A. W. Lazonder and R. Harmsen, "Meta-Analysis of Inquiry-Based Learning: Effects of Guidance," *Review of Educational Research* 86, no. 3 (2016), 681-718; S. Olbrys, "The Deliberative Classroom: Inquiry-Based Teaching, Evaluative Questions, and Deliberation," *Social Education*, 83, no. 1 (January-February 2019), 30-34.

CHAPTER 9

Assessing Inquiry

If you have made it this far in the book, we hope that you have begun to blueprint your curriculum by looping inquiry horizontally across a course of study and that you are working with your colleagues to vertically loop across a series of grade levels. Once you make these moves, meaningful and sustained assessment of inquiry becomes possible. As we demonstrated in the last chapter, students need repeated exposure to and practice with the discrete and interdependent skills developed within an inquiry. Curricular clarity allows teachers to get serious about what they are assessing, what tasks provide evidence of student learning, and how students demonstrate growth over time.

Ultimately, teachers need to answer the question of "how do we know what students know?" and, even more importantly, "how do we know what students know with any degree of confidence?" Educators have struggled with these questions for some time. To be sure, assessing inquiry presents its own challenges. But as the IDM blueprint makes clear, through the distinct but interrelated elements of formative and summative tasks, inquiry-based teachers are in a better position than their more traditional peers to answer the questions above.

In this chapter, we begin by highlighting approaches to assessment and its uses *for* learning, *of* learning, and *as* learning. Then, we turn our attention to the challenges of assessment and how IDM seeks to mitigate those challenges with the task-based structure of the blueprint. We highlight three experimental approaches to assessment using IDM. We end the chapter with a look at design considerations for assessing inquiry and a summary of the affordances and constraints of using IDM as a form of assessment.

Why Assess?
We know that assessing students is murky business and yet, despite all the limitations, we persist with good cause. First and foremost, assessments can enable student agency within a teacher's curriculum—experts call this idea "assessment *for* learning."[1]

Formative assessments, in particular, can provide a steady stream of data to help teachers adjust their instruction to meet their students' needs. For example, if students do not perform well on a particular task, it is incumbent upon the teacher to rethink what she is doing and respond to students' misconceptions.

Assessments also provide students with an opportunity to wrestle with ideas and to demonstrate how they have synthesized their learning. As students interact within a debate, unpack a historical document, construct a map, or create a demand and supply model, they externalize and refine their thinking about a topic. In other words, students can learn material by working through well-constructed assessments. Experts term this situation, "assessment *as* learning."[2]

Teachers are also accountable for reporting the results of students' learning. It is simply unacceptable to tell parents or administrators that, because there is no perfect assessment, we cannot tell them how students are doing in a particular class. Credentialing and certification are part of the educational enterprise and require teachers to ultimately provide "assessments *of* learning."[3]

Despite the challenges of knowing what students know, these purposes of assessment provide us with a call to persist. Because multiple purposes of assessment exist, we must be clear about why we are assessing and what kinds of instruments might help us best achieve our goals. In the following section, we explore the challenge of knowing what students know before turning our attention back to the IDM blueprint and how it can mitigate these challenges.

The Very Real Problem of Assessment

Teaching is hard; learning is hard. Assessment shouldn't be hard; it should be a simple matter of checking for understanding. And with a range of assessment options—class discussion, worksheets, multiple-choice tests, projects—we should be confident that we know what our students know.

And yet assessing what students know, especially with a high degree of confidence, proves to be challenging.[4] We know that high-stakes, standardized tests present a range of problems—a tendency to focus on low-level knowledge, to promote teaching to the test, and to offer little information directly useful to classroom teachers. Classroom-based assessments should be better, more reliable measures of students' learning. Yet problems arise here as well.

One of the biggest problems concerns how students represent what they know and can do.[5] Think about it—how do students demonstrate their abilities? Whether they are answering questions in class, responding to short-answer questions, or making a presentation, they are using language to represent their knowledge and skills. And language, in both its oral and written forms, is a slippery medium.

Another kind of problem surfaces around the context in which students are being assessed. Here, all kinds of factors can interfere with students' ability to show us what they know and can do. Even a short list of these factors—experience with the task, interest in the topic, physical issues (e.g., hunger, lack of sleep, temperature in the room)—suggests how challenging it can be to feel as though we know what students know with any degree of confidence.

One last set of problems involves the nature of assessment itself. A hard truth about assessment is that the form matters. We've all had the experience where we knew an idea cold, yet the way a question was worded threw us off, and we got it wrong. Poorly written questions can undermine students' performance and thus our understanding of it. Still, there is an even nastier dilemma: It turns out that asking students about the same topic but in different formats can show that they know different things.[6] In other words, if we ask students about an historical event through a multiple-choice question, a document-based question, and an oral presentation, we could conclude that they hold very different ideas. This finding suggests that we can assess all we want, but confidence about knowing what students know may be another story.

Each of these problems poses real difficulties. In the following section, however, we respond to some of the real challenges teachers face in assessing students' understanding by highlighting the IDM task structure.

Assessment System in IDM

We have not conquered the problem of assessment with the Inquiry Design Model. But we have installed some features that we think mitigate some of the challenges. In this section, we view the blueprint as an assessment system, breaking it into two major parts and then discussing how these elements address the issues raised in the sections above.

PART I OF THE ASSESSMENT SYSTEM. The first part of the IDM assessment system highlights the relationship between the formative work that surfaces students' knowledge of the supporting questions and the summative work of building evidence-based arguments. Those arguments allow students to synthesize their understandings of the content and to take reasoned positions in response to a compelling question.

A key to this first part of the assessment system is asking students to "show their work." Doing so happens in two ways. First, by pairing every supporting question with a formative performance task, students are continually showing their work and providing teachers with opportunities to assess how their understandings are developing. This information can alert teachers to any emerging problems and can create opportunities to address those problems. A second way that students show their work in an inquiry arises through the connection between the formative and summative tasks. The formative work students do throughout an inquiry helps their teachers feel more confident that they know what their students know. But it is through the summative tasks that students ultimately demonstrate what they know and can do.

Using this approach, the formative work becomes assessment for learning by providing teachers with valuable feedback. That feedback enables teachers to adjust their instruction in response to students' misunderstandings or to create additional practice opportunities before tackling the summative argument task. Many teachers use the summative argument as an assessment of learning as it provides formal feedback to students and parents on how students negotiated a particular inquiry. In the end, it is the arguments that students construct and the claims and evidence they develop to support those arguments that really matter. By holding that goal firmly in mind, teachers can build a coherent image of their students' strengths and weaknesses. Argument making is more than the sum of the formative task parts. But without those formative parts, students' arguments are likely to go astray.

PART II OF THE ASSESSMENT SYSTEM. The second part of the assessment system underscores the work students do after the summative argument. In that work, the key relationships are between the summative argument and the opportunities for extension and taking informed action. The extensions and the informed action possibilities allow students to present adaptations of their arguments to a range of audiences both in and outside the classroom and through a variety of mediums. The informed action activities have an added benefit in that they leverage the civic engagement prospects that the IDM approach offers. In each instance, however, students' arguments figure prominently.

This second part of the assessment system asks students to demonstrate their understandings in a variety of creative venues (e.g., digital documentaries, Socratic discussions, and letters to the editor). But these opportunities are anchored in argumentation such that the ideas are not eclipsed by the modality.[7] Projects, for example, can be a useful avenue for social studies inquiry. And while we are fans of project-based instruction, we firmly believe that projects become more meaningful when students first do the heavy content lifting required by constructing evidence-based arguments. In other words, argumentation acts as a critical formative element of extension and informed action opportunities.

Taken together, these two parts of the IDM assessment system address some of the persistent assessment challenges in social studies. In summary, IDM works to ensure meaningful assessment by:

- Asking students to "show their work" through the progression of formative to summative performance tasks.

- Requiring students to demonstrate their understanding in a variety of modalities (e.g., graphic organizers, claim writing, action opportunities, Socratic discussions).

- Anchoring multi-modal or elaborate assessments in argumentation so the ideas are not eclipsed by the modality. In effect, students' arguments become a critical formative task for summative extensions and action opportunities.

In the next section, we continue our discussion of the assessment system by examining a sixth-grade blueprint on the development of agriculture.

Anatomy of an Assessment System

In order to demonstrate the two components of the IDM assessment system, let's examine a middle-level blueprint with the compelling question, "Was the development of agriculture good for humans?" This question takes advantage of students' intuitive understanding that the development of agriculture was essential and advantageous for humans, but then offers them a chance to explore some of the intended and unintended consequences of this presumed advance. (See Figure 9.1 on page 158.)

FIGURE 9.1: DEVELOPMENT OF AGRICULTURE BLUEPRINT

WAS THE DEVELOPMENT OF AGRICULTURE GOOD FOR HUMANS?

New York State Social Studies Framework Key Idea & Practices	**6.3 EARLY RIVER VALLEY CIVILIZATIONS IN THE EASTERN HEMISPHERE (ca. 3500 BCE – ca. 500 BCE):** Complex societies and civilizations developed in the Eastern Hemisphere. Although these complex societies and civilizations have certain defining characteristics in common, each is also known for unique cultural achievements and contributions. Early human communities in the Eastern Hemisphere adapted to and modified the physical environment. ☑ **Gathering, Using, and Interpreting Evidence** ☑ **Chronological Reasoning and Causation**
Staging the Compelling Question	Make a list of the greatest innovations and write a statement about why particular innovations appear on the list.

Supporting Question 1	Supporting Question 2	Supporting Question 3
How did environmental changes and new technologies affect the development of agriculture?	How did the development of agriculture in Mesopotamia lead to the development of writing?	What were the consequences of agriculture for humans?
Formative Performance Task	**Formative Performance Task**	**Formative Performance Task**
Create a chart with information about how climate change and improved tools contributed to the development of agriculture.	Write a paragraph about how writing emerged in Mesopotamia and describe the implications of that development.	Develop a claim supported by evidence that agriculture had a range of consequences for human culture.
Featured Sources	**Featured Sources**	**Featured Sources**
Source A: Timeline of the Neolithic Revolution **Source B:** Historical temperature data **Source C:** Image bank: Neolithic farming tools	**Source A:** Sumerian counting tokens **Source B:** Sumerian numeric system **Source C:** Clay tablet with cuneiform symbols	**Source A:** Graph of population changes in the Neolithic period **Source B:** Image bank: Life in Paleolithic and Neolithic communities **Source C:** Graph of changes in rates of disease

Summative Performance Task	**ARGUMENT** Was the development of agriculture good for humans? Construct an argument (e.g., detailed outline, poster, or essay) that addresses the compelling question using specific claims and relevant evidence from historical sources while acknowledging competing views.
	EXTENSION Conduct a Socratic dialogue addressing the compelling question.
Taking Informed Action	**UNDERSTAND** Find an example of a modern development (like agriculture) that has resulted in a variety of consequences for humans.
	ASSESS Determine the intended and unintended consequences of the innovation identified.
	ACT Publish a public service announcement about the intended and unintended consequences of the innovation.

The first part of the assessment system features the formative and summative argument tasks. In this inquiry, there are three formative performance tasks that build in sophistication across the blueprint. To respond to those tasks, students examine sources related to the development of agriculture, the emergence of ancient writing in Mesopotamia, and the rise of social inequalities. They also practice the discrete skills of argumentation, including building up content knowledge, writing an explanatory paragraph, and developing an evidence-based claim. This formative work supports students' capacity to construct an argument in response to the compelling question, "Was the development of agriculture good for humans?" (See Figure 9.2)

FIGURE 9.2: PART I OF THE IDM ASSESSMENT SYSTEM

PART I OF THE ASSESSMENT SYSTEM
FORMATIVE TASKS TO SUMMATIVE ARGUMENT

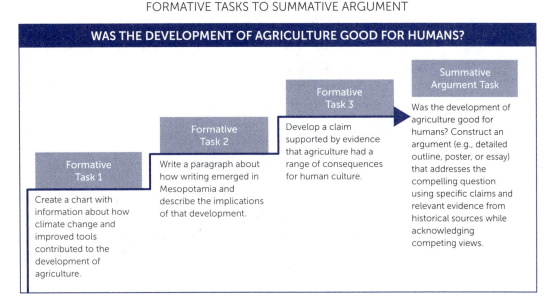

WAS THE DEVELOPMENT OF AGRICULTURE GOOD FOR HUMANS?

Formative Task 1
Create a chart with information about how climate change and improved tools contributed to the development of agriculture.

Formative Task 2
Write a paragraph about how writing emerged in Mesopotamia and describe the implications of that development.

Formative Task 3
Develop a claim supported by evidence that agriculture had a range of consequences for human culture.

Summative Argument Task
Was the development of agriculture good for humans? Construct an argument (e.g., detailed outline, poster, or essay) that addresses the compelling question using specific claims and relevant evidence from historical sources while acknowledging competing views.

Teachers can learn all kinds of things by looking at students' responses to the tasks individually and together. Looking at them individually, the formative tasks help teachers understand their students' abilities to navigate new and familiar concepts and skills while the summative task helps teachers evaluate their students' abilities to synthesize the understandings that develop across an inquiry. In the agriculture inquiry, the formative tasks show whether or not students are gaining the kind of content knowledge (e.g., the impact of climate and technology on agriculture and the emergence of writing as a form of communication) and disciplinary skills (e.g., synthesizing information and writing evidence-based claims) they need in order to develop and support their arguments.

Turning now to students' performances on an inquiry's formative and summative tasks, teachers can pinpoint existing and emerging strengths and challenges. For example, are students able to articulate an argument that actually addresses the compelling question? Do their claims build out their argument? Do they use evidence from the sources in ways that support their claims? Constructing thoughtful arguments is a challenging task with all kinds of opportunities for mayhem to ensue. But by looking at how students handle the formative tasks and then move toward the summative experience, teachers are better able to diagnose when and where students go off the rails.

Part II of the IDM assessment system emerges when we look at the relationship between the summative argument and the extension and taking informed action activities. (See Figure 9.3)

Because an extension offers students an opportunity to cast their arguments in a new form, the linkage between these two elements should be tight. And yet, it isn't always. Students may think that they are faithfully representing their arguments in an extension activity, but teachers may detect areas where students' responses to the two tasks are out of sync. For example, students who provide evidence to support their stance on the question of the value of agriculture may forget to do so during a Socratic debate.

Students' arguments also need to figure into their activities when they take informed action. With the development of agricultural inquiry, the simplest illustration of this idea occurs when students are able to identify current situations that yield a mix of intended and unintended consequences. Elements of their arguments should also surface in the steps where they assess and act. If their arguments are generally sound, then it is unlikely that students will completely miss the boat on the informed action sequence. But alert teachers may well see discrepancies that can turn into teachable moments.

There is one more element of the IDM assessment system worth noting here. For while we see value in looking at the relationship between formative and summative tasks and between students' arguments and their efforts at extension and informed action, there is particular value in looking at students' formative and summative work across the school year.

If teachers are doing at least a couple of inquiries throughout the year, they have an opportunity to evaluate their students' growth over time and experience. In this sense, then, the formative and summative work students do in one inquiry become formative for the next one. What teachers learn about their students' knowledge and skill development in the first inquiry can inform the development and assessment of tasks in subsequent inquiries. Thus, the examples of horizontal looping we described in Chapter 8 also serve the purpose of a teacher's assessment program. And if a school or district employs a vertical looping strategy, then teachers across

PART II OF THE ASSESSMENT SYSTEM
SUMMATIVE ARGUMENT TO EXTENSION/TAKING INFORMED ACTION

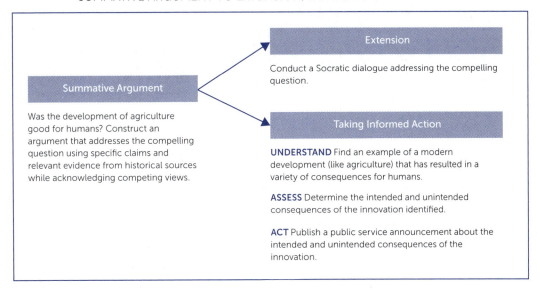

grade levels should be able to chart and understand their students' progress and then develop instructional interventions aimed at helping their students hone their argumentation skills.

The Assessment System in Action

As we discussed in chapter 8, inquiry as a curricular approach becomes coherent when it loops across a course of study and even more so when it loops across grade levels. We say this because when a group of teachers commits to inquiry, they also commit to emphasizing the skills that are foundational to inquiry—questioning, sourcing, argumentation, communication, and action. These essential skills become the north star of the social studies curriculum. That's a powerful idea for social studies as teachers are able to calibrate their assessment criteria to focus on the content *and* the skills of inquiry. And, once committed to looping inquiry, teachers can begin to see students' skill development and growth over time as they practice the same set of important skills in a variety of content contexts.

As we travel across the country and interact with teachers implementing IDM inquiries, we come across interesting and ambitious classroom grading approaches to inquiry. We would need an entire book to discuss them all and we are almost at the end of this one! So, here, we briefly describe three innovations that have stood out. The first approach focuses on evaluating the quality of an evidentiary claim. The second involves students developing a single-point rubric around the summative argument. The third approach tackles inquiry skills and a standards-based grading reporting system. Taken together, we think these examples provide guidance around first steps teachers may want to take when thinking about assessing inquiry and the relationship between looping inquiry and assessment.

What's in a Claim?

A group of high school teachers from four different schools in Lexington, Kentucky have been using IDM for several years, looping it throughout their courses. But they started to experience a problem when trying to improve students' claim making. They asked themselves these questions: How do I help students construct better claims? How should I describe a claim in student-friendly language? How can my feedback on claim-making become more meaningful for students? These teachers got to work by collaborating on the following description for evidentiary claims, which includes four characteristics that they find give their students an understanding of what makes a "good" claim.

The teachers began by defining claims and describing their function. They wrote that a claim is an "assertion supported by factual information and evidence from sources." They describe four characteristics of claims as persuasive, reasoned, clear, and accurate. (See Figure 9.4)

These teachers are in the process of testing this model out in their classrooms using student claims, but before they did, they wanted to ensure that they themselves could parse a claim according to these characteristics. They used a tenth-grade IDM inquiry on the French Revolution to beta-test their framework. Focusing on the supporting question "Did Napoleon's rise to power represent a continuation of or an end to revolutionary ideals?" the teachers drafted the following evidentiary claim:

> Even though Napoleon's rise to power brought about order and an attempt at reform through his Code Napoleon, his reign was not a continuation of the Revolution due to his consolidation of power as Emperor and the suppression of critics and the press in France.

They then worked together to test their claim according to the characteristics. If they couldn't do it, they knew they couldn't expect students to do it. What follows is their analysis:

FIGURE 9.4. DESCRIPTION OF AN EVIDENTIARY CLAIM

ON THE NATURE OF CLAIMS			
An *evidentiary claim* is an assertion that is supported with factual information and evidence from sources. A claim is often written in one or two sentences as the claim is meant to state conclusions and not necessarily to be explanatory/expository. Claims can be a response to a question or they can be deduced by examining source(s). In either case, the key is that the claim is supported by the evidence that the student has interpreted and excerpted from sources regardless of the conflicting nature and/or complexity of the source(s).			
Persuasive	**Reasoned**	**Clear**	**Accurate**
A *persuasive* evidentiary claim should be a convincing statement expressing a "weighty" evidentiary stance. Highly persuasive claims are supported with corroborating evidence and should account for evidentiary discrepancies.	A *reasoned* evidentiary claim should be logical and valid. Such a claim demonstrates students' thoughtful interpretation of sources in relationship to a question or task.	A *clear* evidentiary claim should use clear and objective language to effectively communicate conclusions. Clarity allows the claim to speak to a wide audience who may not have examined the same sources as the author.	An *accurate* evidentiary claim presents factual information that is verifiable, is accepted as true, and reflects a plausible interpretation of a source(s). Such a claim is relevant to the question at hand and reflects a clear understanding of the relevant ideas and events.

Persuasive: This claim is "persuasive" because it weighs evidence. Napoleon was a "child" of the Enlightenment and believed in many liberal reforms. This point was taken into consideration, but it was weighed against Napoleon's actions as Emperor. The claim was informed by multiple sources of information.

Reasoned: The claim is "reasoned" in that it answers and considers all parts of the question. The claim shows an attempt to arrive at a conclusion that is supported by the evidence. The claim is valid as it follows an historical attempt at comparing one series of events to another, looking for similarities or differences.

Clear: The claim is "clear" in that it uses language that is objective and clear. The author uses content specific vocabulary in order to add specificity, avoiding vague allusions to events or individuals.

Accurate: This claim is "accurate" in that all of the actions mentioned in the claim are accepted as true and are both verifiable by and reasonably inferred from primary and secondary sources. The Code Napoleon was an actual law enforced in France that many historians recognize as important and significant. Napoleon did crown himself Emperor. There are several letters written by Napoleon discussing his political ideals showing that he was influenced by Enlightenment thought.

As we write this book, these teachers now are pressure testing their model with students' claims and hope to publish a final version of their criteria soon. In the meantime, we give these teachers an enthusiastic C3 Teachers shout out for leading the way on meaningful assessment of one of the key components of IDM, claim-making.

What Makes a Good Argument?

A second notable assessment innovation also comes from a high school classroom in Kentucky. Ryan New has brought students into the assessment process around argumentation. In his classroom, students complete 10-12 inquiries a year. Mr. New relies heavily on focused inquiries, but uses structured and student-directed inquiries as well. Because inquiry is looped with such frequency, students become very familiar with constructing arguments in response to compelling questions. To improve their arguments over the year, Mr. New introduced students to the single-point rubric.

The single-point rubric is a set of assessment criteria that serve as benchmarks. (See Figure 9.5) The column to the left of the criteria is labeled *detractors* and the one to the right is labeled *enhancers*. Detractors are those things students do that take away from their arguments. For example, an argument that includes inaccurate information detracts from the claims that a student is making. An enhancer is just the opposite. Students may use a particularly poignant quote at the beginning of an argument that strengthens their overall position. The idea behind the detractor-enactor structure is that teachers can assess student work more organically, meaning that they can be open to the ways in which students exceed or fail to meet the criteria.

Many of us have a love-hate relationship with grading rubrics. Veteran teachers know there is always some degree of fudge factor when grading with a rubric and they can feel confined by a rubric once they encounter students' ideas on paper. Students can surprise us with insights that aren't captured in the rubric or alternatively throw us a curveball we hadn't imagined when we designed the task and/or the rubric.

To address these points, Mr. New asked his high school students to draft a rubric after completing their first IDM in the course. The students examined the work they did on the first inquiry, conducted peer reviews, and worked together to develop the criteria so they could do better on the subsequent inquiries. (See Figure 9.5) That is IDM innovation at its best!

ARGUMENTATIVE RUBRIC		
Detractors	Criteria	Enhancers
	Introduction and conclusion establish the context and scope of the response and reflect the tone of the paper. 10 POINTS	
	Thesis responds to a compelling question, champions a position with established, well-reasoned categories. 15 POINTS	
	Claims are supported with relevant evidence from a variety of credible sources and are congruent with thesis. Claims are clear, complex, and sophisticated. 25 POINTS	
	Evidence is carefully analyzed and explained so that intepretations and conclusions consistently reflect understanding and logic. 25 POINTS	
	Overall argument is logically organized; language effectively expresses ideas; grammar and syntax is appropriate; response is consistent in delivery; evidence is properly and seamlessly cited. 15 POINTS	
	Audience is engaged throughout argument and delivery. 10 POINTS	
	TOTAL POINTS:	
COMMENTS:		

The single-point rubric provides a consistent set of valuable criteria that describes what we are looking for in a summative task. It also allows teachers to offer constructive feedback to their students.

In IDM, we think these benefits have particular resonance. Social studies does not follow a series of learning progressions that are common to subjects like math and reading. We build competency in social studies by repeating the same set of skills over and over again, using different content to practice those skills. Student competency in social studies, then, represents a cumulative quality as students are able to hone the skills acquired within one inquiry and transfer those skills to the content of another inquiry—think IDM looping!

It is important to note that within a course of study, a student's performance can be uneven both within an inquiry and across inquiries. For example, one student might demonstrate competency in one or two criteria and not others. Another student might master all the criteria in one inquiry, but then slip in his performance on a subsequent inquiry. In determining competency, teachers need to consider the preponderance of evidence over a number of inquiry experiences when evaluating their students at the end of an inquiry. This approach becomes particularly important when IDM meets standards-based or competency-based grading models such as the one we describe in the next section.

What's in a Social Studies Grade?

As we stated in the last chapter, looping sets teachers up for meaningful assessment, grading, and reporting. This is good news for schools, departments, and districts that are moving to proficiency-based, competency-based, and/or standards-based grading (SBG) and reporting models. In each of these models, teachers determine a common set of criteria to report student progress. Social studies educators often resist developing criteria because we struggle to pinpoint the content and skills that loop in a course, and then across courses. As we discussed in the last chapter, IDM allows this criterion setting to become much more apparent. If fourth, eighth, and twelfth grade teachers are all having students read and evaluate sources, craft evidentiary claims and arguments, express these arguments in a variety of mediums, and take informed action, we begin to see common criteria emerge.

One such district in Bloomington, Illinois is on the cutting edge with an IDM social studies curriculum and a new standards-based grading model. A district-wide push for ambitious instruction

FIGURE 9.6: AN EXAMPLE OF REPORTING STRANDS AND PRIORITY TARGETS FOR INQUIRY-BASED SOCIAL STUDIES.

Strand 1: Perspectives	**Priority Target 1:** Identify the role of individuals, groups, and institutions in peoples' struggle for safety, freedom, equality and justice.
	Priority Target 2: Analyze key historical events and contributions of individuals through a variety of perspectives, including those of historically underrepresented groups.
Strand 2: Causation and Argumentation	**Priority Target 3:** Analyze multiple and complex causes and effects of events in the past.
Strand 3: Evaluating Sources and Using Evidence	**Priority Target 4:** Gather and evaluate information from multiple sources while considering the origin, credibility, point of view, authority, structure, context, and corroborative value of the sources.
	Priority Target 5: Identify evidence that draws information from multiple sources to revise or strengthen claims.
Strand 4: Communicating Conclusions	**Priority Target 6:** Construct and evaluate explanations and arguments using multiple sources and relevant, verified information.
	Priority Target 7: Articulate explanations and arguments to a targeted audience in diverse settings.

around inquiry is coupled with a simultaneous push for better grading and reporting through a standards-based grading model. These teachers began innovating in the eleventh grade because they were already looping inquiry in an assigned U.S. History course. They were able to pinpoint four reporting strands for their report card: (1) perspectives; (2) causation and argumentation; (3) evaluating sources and using evidence; and (4) communicating conclusions. Additionally, they developed seven "priority targets" that defined the strand and the focus for student achievement within the strand. (See Figure 9.6)

Using six required common assessments across all sections of the U.S. History course, the teachers were able to track where students encountered each priority target. It is no surprise that we like their model a lot because they are using IDM as their common assessments. But even more important, this approach is really the holy grail of social studies—a coherent social studies program that uses inquiry as the connective thread between standards, curriculum, instruction, and assessment. (See Figure 9.7)

FIGURE 9.7: INQUIRY AT THE CENTER OF SOCIAL STUDIES STANDARDS, CURRICULUM, INSTRUCTION, AND ASSESSMENT.

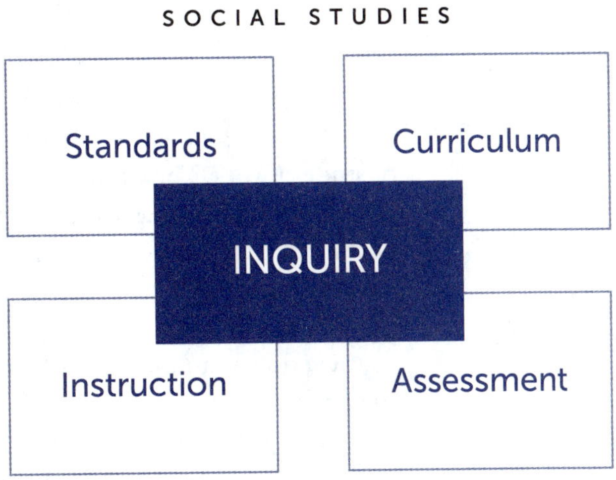

SOCIAL STUDIES

Standards	Curriculum
INQUIRY	
Instruction	Assessment

Design Considerations

This chapter is not intended to tackle every issue around assessment. We think of assessment as we do a hydra, the many-headed serpent from Greek mythology. Taking on assessment often feels like cutting off one head only for another (and another) to appear. Although assessment is vexing, our hope is to point inquiry-minded teachers in useful directions. We think that some of the innovations we highlight in this chapter are a good place to start. Below we detail some design considerations for those brave enough to take on the assessment hydra!

DON'T START WITH ASSESSMENT—GET COMFORTABLE WITH INQUIRY FIRST! Educators often want to practice extreme makeovers in schools. We get it—social studies sometimes needs a serious update. But, meaningful change has to be thoughtful and strategic.

Teachers can get burned out when reform movements rush in and out of their schools, and asking them to do too much at one time only exacerbates this fatigue.

Our recommendation around inquiry is to start by trying out a curricular inquiry—an existing one or one of your own design. Then, try teaching a second or even a third one before tackling assessment. Our experience tells us that folks who are doing really innovative assessment work have committed to inquiry and are in it for the long game. Each example we highlighted above represents teachers who experimented with inquiry for some time before they took on the assessment challenge. Our suggestion is that social studies coordinators, department chairs, and individual teachers build an on-ramp for inquiry that allows teachers to accelerate over time.

YOU MAY NOT WANT TO GRADE IT ALL. One of the biggest affordances and challenges with inquiry is that it produces a lot of student work. For example, a structured inquiry can produce 7 pieces of student work from the 3-4 formative and 2-3 summative performance tasks. That number multiplied by the number of students can create a quite a bit of information on student progress.

So, how do you manage all of that evidence of learning? One suggestion we make is to think about grading efficiencies with the formative work, focusing the heavy-duty grading on the summative work. For example, consider using in-class feedback strategies for the formative performance tasks. Teachers we have talked to have used peer review, whole group review, and quick check-ins to ensure students are tracking with the material and moving productively forward toward the summative work. We applaud teachers when they find efficient ways to honor students' work and keep their heads above water when doing inquiry!

Affordances and Constraints of a Guided Inquiry

Assessment and grading expert Rick Stiggins writes, "students can hit any target that they know about and that stands still for them."[8] IDM helps teachers to set a consistent set of targets around skills that are essential to inquiry. But, even when those targets are clear, assessing student work is far from simple. Assessment involves a set of complicated factors including assessment validity, students' experiences and motivation with the task, and the ever-present challenge of ever really knowing what students actually know. With all these imperfections, social studies educators need a systematic assessment system that helps to mitigate the challenges and to amplify the outcomes of a meaningful social studies education. In the table below, we summarize the affordances and constraints of using IDM as the foundation for an assessment system.

TABLE 9.1: AFFORDANCES AND CONSTRAINTS OF USING IDM AS THE FOUNDATION FOR AN ASSESSMENT SYSTEM

ASSESSING INQUIRY	
Affordances	Constraints
Asks students to "show their work" through the progression of formative to summative performance tasks.	Produces a lot of student work and teachers need to be thoughtful about their grading approaches.
Requires students to demonstrate their understandings in a variety of modalities (e.g., graphic organizers, claim writing, action opportunities, Socratic discussions).	Demands that teachers realize the challenges that quality assessment brings
Anchors multi-modal or elaborate assessments in argumentation so the ideas are not eclipsed by modality (e.g., arguments become a critical formative task for summative extensions and action opportunities).	Changes may not happen overnight. Teachers may need an "on-ramp" with inquiry in order to tackle a systematic assessment approach.
Provides a "North Star" for inquiry skills that recur across a course of study.	

Conclusion

In the next chapter, we zoom back out to take a wide-angle view of the Inquiry Design Model. Using questions, tasks, and sources as our lens, we discuss IDM as a way of thinking and work to connect to other inquiry-based models (e.g., Project-Based Learning) and with other disciplines.

NOTES

1. R. Stiggins and J. Chappuis, *An Introduction to Student-Involved Assessment for Learning*, 6th edition (Upper Saddle River, NJ: Pearson, 2012); G. Wiggins, *Educative Assessment: Designing Assessments to Inform and Improve Student Performance* (San Francisco: Jossey-Bass, 1998).

2. L. M. Earl, *Assessment as Learning: Using Classroom Assessment to Maximize Student Learning*, 2nd edition (Thousand Oaks, CA: Corwin Press, 2012).

3. G. Wiggins, *Educative Assessment: Designing Assessments to Inform and Improve Student Performance*.

4. S. G. Grant, "The Problem with Knowing What Students Know: Classroom-Based and Large-Scale Assessment in Social Studies," in C. Bolick and M. M. Manfra (Eds.), *Handbook of Social Studies Research* (New York: Wiley-Blackwell, 2016), 461-476.

5. S. G. Grant, "Understanding What Children Know about History: Exploring the Representation and Testing Dilemmas," *Social Studies Research and Practice* 2, no. 2 (2007), 196-208. Available online at http://www.socstrp.org.

6. G. Nuthall and A. Alton-Lee, "Assessing Classroom Learning: How Students Use Their Knowledge and Experience to Answer Classroom Achievement Test Questions in Science and Social Studies," *American Educational Research Journal* 32, no. 1 (1995), 185-223; B. VanSledright, T. Kelly, and K. Meuwissen, "Oh, the Trouble We Have Seen: Researching Historical Thinking and Understanding," in K. Barton (Ed.), *Research Methods in Social Studies Education* (Greenwich, CT: Information Age Publishing, 2006), 207-233.

7. K. Swan and M. Hofer, "Examining Student-Created Documentaries as a Mechanism for Engaging Students in Authentic Intellectual Work," *Theory and Research in Social Education* 41, no. 1 (2013), 133-175.

8. R. Stiggins, *Revolutionize Assessment: Empower Students, Inspire Learning* (New York: Corwin, 2014), 32.

CHAPTER 10

IDM As a Way of Thinking

IDM is not just an approach to designing instruction or curriculum scaffolding for supporting inquiry in social studies; it's a way of thinking. When thinking with IDM, *questions, tasks,* and *sources* lead the way. With questions in mind, teachers put students first by respecting their interests and by honoring their efforts to learn with inquiry. IDM thinking is task-based when teachers engage with students at every twist and turn in the learning process, assessing their progress and supporting their emerging understandings. IDM thinking also goes to the source by keeping content and disciplinary knowledge in the forefront.

Improving education is at the core of IDM thinking. Whether it is designing an inquiry-centered curriculum, designing the instructional implementation of an inquiry plan, or designing the assessment of student learning in an inquiry, when working with IDM, teachers are aiming to lift up the experiences of their students. As a way of thinking, IDM is oriented toward solving educational problems. This problem-solving focus is driven by teachers' attention to their students' interest (as represented in questions), their understanding of pedagogy and assessment (represented in the tasks), and their knowledge of content and attention to the disciplines (sources). Attention to these matters is what we mean when we say that questions, tasks, and sources are at the core of IDM thinking.

IDM thinking is a different way to approach education, but this way of thinking is not blind to or dismissive of other approaches to teaching and learning. We are often asked how IDM fits with other approaches to student-centered learning such as Project-Based Learning (PBL) and Document-Based Questions (DBQ). Our answer is that IDM fits well. It is in line with the student-centered nature of these other instructional approaches. However, IDM is not just an instructional approach; it is also a way of thinking about teaching and learning. Teachers also ask us if they can use IDM in other school subjects such as the arts, English, mathematics, and science. The answer there is a definitive yes. IDM works in any school subject as long as (1) questions are worth asking and answering in those other courses, (2) the tasks are useful as a way to respond to the questions, and (3) there are sources that enable students to complete the tasks.

In this chapter, we expand on our ideas about IDM as a way of thinking with questions, tasks, and sources toward the goal of solving educational problems. We also examine other approaches to student-centered learning, and the ways IDM works across the school subjects.

Solving Problems Through IDM Thinking

The Inquiry Design Model originated as an effort to put the C3 Framework's Inquiry Arc into instructional motion as expressed through the 10 steps in the IDM Design Path.[1] Learning from innovative teachers using IDM in their classrooms, we have come to view IDM as more than just the steps in the design process or the efforts teachers make when implementing inquiry. We now see IDM as a way of thinking rooted in a larger design-thinking ethos. IDM thinking is about solving educational problems.

Goldman and Kabayadondo describe designing as, above all else, a commitment to solving problems. In education, they see design thinking as a fluid and dynamic process:

> Design thinking has been visualized in many ways; most involve a user-centered, empathy driven approach aimed at creating solutions through gaining insight into people's needs. Design thinking also involves creating conceptual (and sometimes working) prototypes that get improved through feedback and testing with stakeholders. Learning with design thinking often starts with the method. The aim is to move beyond merely going through the steps of the process and to develop mindset change experiences such as empathy development, participation in "team collaborations," commitment to action-oriented problem-solving, a sense of efficacy, and understanding that failure and persistence to try again after failures are necessary and productive aspects of success.[2]

Following on Goldman and Kabayadondo's description of designing, the IDM way of thinking is user-centered. Students as "users" are always on our minds when we develop and implement inquiry lessons. IDM thinking is empathetic, as the point of view of students rather than teachers is the priority. IDM thinking is also solution-oriented. It takes on the immediate learning needs of students by considering their interests and being respectful of their intellectual capacities, while also taking on larger curriculum issues that can constrain students.

In Chapter 1, we ask why inquiry is not the norm in classrooms. Researchers tell us that inquiry-based practice is good for students. They can do the work and they revel in it. So, what's the problem? We identified several persistent issues limiting inquiry—teachers' lack of experience with inquiry, the limits of time to design and implement inquiry, and large-scale assessments that encourage traditional teacher-centered instruction—to name a few. IDM as a way of thinking takes on each of these three problems. In the sections that follow, we examine these problems and describe the ways that IDM thinking creates solutions.

Building Up Teachers' Experiences with Inquiry Design

Teachers' lack of experience with inquiry may hold some back, including even those ambitious teachers who want to do more but are limited in their opportunities to experience inquiry. Thirty years ago, the Holmes Group identified curriculum knowledge as a critical part of the process of improving the quality of education in our schools and the quality of the teachers within these schools.[3] In the years since, the curriculum landscape around schools and teachers has shifted in dramatic ways. The move to standardized curriculum driven by the Common Core, Next Generation Science Standards, and the C3 Framework is opening up opportunities for teachers to innovate with curriculum in the classroom as states and districts implement standards-aligned curriculum packages. At the same time, the curriculum development field has flattened with new open-source platforms and opportunities for curricular customization. What are teachers to do in this dynamic curricular environment?

Perhaps now more than ever, teachers have an opportunity to participate directly in curriculum reform. Although they might not be on the front lines of *standards* development, teachers can play an important role. In our experience of building inquiries, we see teachers as leading the *curriculum* development work. The impact comes with implementation when inquiries designed with IDM are shared across a school, district, or state. That's why we established C3 Teachers to enable this sort of dissemination and scaling up of inquiry. This work of scaling up inquiry curriculum cannot happen if teachers are not equipped with the dispositions and ways of thinking that support inquiry teaching. IDM thinking repositions teachers as designers empowered to solve their instructional problems and puts them on a path toward becoming more knowledgeable about and confident with inquiry. This is the long game of IDM. It's not just building inquiries; it's their implementation in classrooms. And there it is the mindset of teachers that matters. IDM teachers use inquiry to privilege those questions that matter for students, to enable their work on those questions with thoughtful tasks, and to empower students with sources that deliver the content to bring inquiry to life.

C3 Teachers takes on the problem of teachers not having experience with inquiry by empowering them to participate in curriculum reform work; such efforts are at the core of all that C3 Teachers does. The C3 Teachers network enables teachers to learn together through professional development and to work together to build inquiries and implement them in their classrooms. C3 Teachers leverages all of this work through an open-source online publishing platform to enlarge the base of educators who are experiencing with inquiry. The network is taking on the problem of teachers' lack of experience with inquiry by enabling their participation in curriculum reform. But this is just the starting point. Within the overall body of curriculum work, IDM thinking is creating solutions in many other areas related to inquiry learning.

Taking on the Tyranny of Time

For teachers to participate in curriculum reform is a great idea, but we are not naïve about it. A willingness to design and use inquiry in the classroom and a supportive network may not be enough. Even when teachers commit to inquiry, there are secondary barriers to doing inquiry. We all must work to mitigate these constraints and, with collective effort, progress can and will come. But, there is one limitation that seems to loom even more ominously than these—the constraint of time.

We are familiar with and sympathetic to the lament of teachers that if they had more time, they would use more inquiry. We think that this is a manageable problem and one where IDM as a way of thinking can be enormously helpful. What we have found is that, in the end, inquiry is no more or less time intensive that any other approach to teaching. It's just another variable to be dealt with in the design process.

When thinking as designers committed to solving the problem of time in the curriculum, we can focus on the elements of the problem that are holding us back. If the problem is that it takes too much time to read the sources in an inquiry, then we carefully select excerpts to convey the content needed. That's what was on our mind when we wrote about "preparing" sources:

> It is rare that a source, as created, is perfectly suited for use in an inquiry. Because most of the sources in inquiries are being placed into duty as interpretative materials for students, changes to the sources are often necessary. Some sources, such as photographs, may be used "as is" in an inquiry, but most sources require adaptation.[4] This process of adapting sources for use in an inquiry can take three forms—excerpting, modifying, and annotating.[5]

As designers, we identified the problem of time as being a constraint and, with the needs of students in mind, we worked toward a solution that emphasized the preparation of sources for an inquiry. Excerpts, modifications, and annotations position sources so that students are able to engage them and not stall in frustration or overcommit the limited time we have in the curriculum.

The preparation of sources addresses the problem of how much time is needed to read a source, but what if the problem is more comprehensive? What if the number of days that are available to work on an inquiry topic is limited? A response to that problem is to pare down the number of tasks. That's actually the thinking that led to the focused inquiry model presented in this book. It sounds simple, but it takes a lot of design effort to build a focused inquiry that represents all the elements of an inquiry while also saving instructional time. Other ways to address the problem may be to actually remove elements of the inquiry. And that's O.K! The Inquiry Design Model is modular in nature. As long as the core tasks that enable students to encounter a compelling question and respond with an argument are in place, then all the other elements are modular. Those include the staging task, the extension task, and even that of taking informed action.

Time constrains everything that we do, whether it's the lack of time to design inquiry or the lack of time in the curriculum to teach inquiry. Other constraints are also in place. Next, we look at assessment as another problem to be overcome with IDM thinking.

Promoting Assessment through Inquiry

Large-scale assessments, the sort of assessments implemented to hold teachers accountable and to provide common measures for student success are a powerful driver of how teachers engage students. We see the power of these assessments play out in all school subjects where a standardized test can drive teaching and learning in ways that are counter to our best instincts. If these assessments appear to push teachers toward traditional teaching methods, then inquiry gets squeezed.

So, what is an inquiry-minded teacher to do? For one thing, be secure in knowing that assessment and instruction are inseparable. As such, teachers can begin to claim the assessment mandate by making it clear that through their everyday instruction they are generating the assessment data that schools and systems can use to accomplish the goals of accountability.

As we describe in chapter 9, IDM takes on the assessment problem by putting forward an assessment model through the task-based structure of the blueprint, with formative and summative assessments hard-wired into the document. By doing so, IDM is putting forward an approach to teaching and learning with inquiry that is an assessment system. Those ideas about assessment did not just emerge from thin air. This assessment work is a direct application of IDM thinking. When we think with questions, tasks, and sources in mind, we come to see how opportunities for repeated practice with content and skills become possible, thus driving classroom, departmental, district-wide common assessments, and even state-wide assessments. By taking on the problem of assessment, we are able to realize that learning through IDM is a formative and summative assessment experience.

We shared several examples of how assessment is realized through the IDM structure in Chapter 9. With each of these examples, we put forward a solution to one of the most vexing problems facing teachers today—how can classroom teachers own assessment, produce high- quality information for making decisions about student growth, and generate data for their own accountability? We may not have completely cracked the assessment puzzle, but by engaging in IDM thinking we have a better chance than not of making progress.

The following examples of IDM thinking offer a clear message: Design thinking in education is oriented toward solving instructional problems and teachers are at the forefront of that process.

IDM in the Big Curriculum Picture

As we noted in Chapter 1, inquiry has a long history in education. From John Dewey's advocacy of inquiry learning as a way to promote democratic life, to our latest efforts to connect learning in social studies to civic life through the C3 Framework, inquiry has been a mainstay of our rhetoric about schooling. Curricular approaches such as the New Social Studies and *Man: A Course of Study* in the 1960s, and more recently Project-Based Learning and an emphasis on Document-Based Questions (DBQ) by the College Board, are all antecedent to IDM.

Situated in this legacy, IDM shares much with these historical and contemporary approaches. However, there are some important points of departure. IDM aims to take on the whole of inquiry. It seeks to establish a theory of inquiry-based thinking that includes the design of instruction, the implementation of inquiry plans, and the assessment of student learning—and it situates all of those efforts as a way of thinking. In this section, we review some other approaches to inquiry with IDM in mind.

IDM and Other Approaches to Inquiry

As a curriculum model, IDM draws from existing curriculum models and shares many commonalities with some of the best known of these approaches. Project-Based Learning, Document-Based Questions, and the Learning Design Collaborative all represent aspects of the components of IDM. (See Table 10.1 on page 178.)

In emphasizing questions, IDM and Project-Based Learning (PBL) are quite similar. The Buck Institute's widely adopted PBL model centers on a challenging problem or question that students examine through sustained inquiry leading to a public product. The Document-Based Question model is also driven by questions and, like IDM, involves close analysis of disciplinary sources. And as with IDM, the Learning Design Collaborative (LDC) model places an emphasis on task-based work and opportunities for students to build up their literacy skills.

TABLE 10.1: IDM AND OTHER CURRICULUM MODELS

CURRICULUM APPROACH	LEADING MODEL	CONNECTION TO IDM
Project-Based Learning (PBL)	Buck Institute www.pblworks.org	Questions drive students' engagement with academic content.
Document-Based Questions	DBQ Project www.dbqproject.com	Disciplinary source work provides students with access to content.
Literacy-Based Practices	Learning Design Collaborative www.ldc.org	Task-based exercises provide students with opportunities to practice with literacy skills.

The similarities between IDM and other curriculum models are not a coincidence. In building the Inquiry Design Model, we sought out the most innovative approaches and practices to support student learning. In our first IDM book, we describe these connections in depth.[6] We also made the point that consistency across inquiry models is good for education. Even the most ambitious teachers may feel a bit jaded by claims of a new curriculum innovation promising radical change. With IDM, we make a case for the next big thing being the thing you already know about, just packaged in a more comprehensive and coherent manner, one that is simple to access and robust in application. Most good teachers know and appreciate inquiry. They just get jumbled in their thoughts when models don't talk to one another or when they make exclusive promises. In contrast, teachers can think with IDM in mind and understand other curriculum models. If you understand IDM, the focus on questions in PBL makes sense. The DBQ emphasis on sources is completely logical if you have your IDM thinking cap on. And when you value the task-based structure of IDM, the LDC model makes perfect sense. In fact, all of these models and more fit in an overall gestalt of inquiry that is the IDM way of thinking.

IDM Across the Disciplines

Right up there with questions about how IDM fits with other curriculum models are questions about whether IDM works in other curriculum areas. We are social studies educators, and IDM was an intentional effort to bring the ideas in the C3 Framework to instructional life. However, in the process of developing IDM, we had other curriculum areas in mind. Doing so made sense given that social studies is, in many ways, the heart of the school curriculum. We know that social studies might not receive as much time in the curriculum or as much attention in the testing regimes or, regrettably, in funding for research and innovation, but perhaps that's because social studies is so deeply embedded in other school subjects. After all, social studies shares as its core purpose the purpose of schooling in general—to prepare young people for productive and effective life in our democratic society. Social studies enables students to build up their oral and written skills. Work in social studies enables students to make and support arguments with implications for science and technology, for how societies change and how the arts demonstrate ways that people make sense of their lives and find joy. In social studies, we do it all! It is the heart of the curriculum and we think that the inquiry pedagogy that brings social studies to life is relevant for all school subject areas.

The arrangement of school subjects by academic disciplines has many advantages (e.g., curriculum development, preparation of teachers, and teaching of disciplinary skills), but when these subjects become isolated, the result can be crippling for the overall aims of school. Having all teachers on board with the mission of the schools as well as the key instructional methods that drive that mission is essential. But it's not just within the silos of the disciplines that inquiry should flourish. We know that the best questions emerge from the messy borders and overlapping spaces that disciplines occupy. Here are a few examples:

The compelling question, "What Do Family Stories Tell Us About the Past?" draws together history and sociology.

"Was the Development of Agriculture Good for Humans?" pulls on economics, history, and archaeology.

"Did the Chinese and Romans Know Each Other?" requires the study of geography and history.

"Do Any Political Parties Represent Me?" enables a blend of psychology and political science.

We just pulled these four compelling questions randomly from our collection of over 300 inquiries. We are convinced that all compelling questions enable a blending of disciplines. We invite you to test that out yourself!

This sort of inquiry landscape is rarely experienced in disciplinary silos and is just as rarely experienced by students in schools. Through multi-disciplinary approaches to teaching and learning, however, we can help students make connections to the world around them and be better prepared for college and career.[7] That is IDM thinking at it best—questions that emerge from students' experiences, sources that reflect content generated in the ongoing activities of people in the world, and tasks that are opportunities to do the things that are valued in work and life. Those are the core principles that define IDM thinking.

In our work with teachers, we have seen some disciplinary border crossings in practice. In a science inquiry on nuclear power that links to the Kentucky Science Standards, Andrea New from Louisville, Kentucky asked the compelling question, "Is nuclear power worth the risk?" (See Figure 10.1) This inquiry draws on a powerful combination of science-related sources to take on a critically important question in social studies.

In another inquiry with a math focus that links to the Common Core State Standards for Math, one of our teacher partners featured the compelling question "What's the best way to buy that PlayStation?" (See Figure 10.2 on page 182.) This inquiry provides students with a real-world scenario that has multiple "right" answers, but requires the use and application of algebraic concepts and routines.

IDM was born in social studies, but from the beginning has had implications for all school subjects. The focus on questions, tasks, and sources resonates with teachers in every discipline and IDM provides these teachers with a consistent way to empower students to learn in every subject in authentic ways.

Final Thoughts

We recognize that IDM cannot be all things to all people. It is a model that has some things to say about the way students learn best and the ways that teachers can best facilitate students' learning. IDM is active, student-focused, and connected to our civic experiences. If you don't buy these ideas, then IDM will not resonate with you. However, we think that the time is right for these big curriculum ideas. With increased coherence resulting from national standards projects, now seems to be the time. With the leveling of the curriculum playing field through open-source publishing, now seems to be the time. With a growing willingness of teachers to seize the levers of power in schools and districts to fight for what they believe is best for their students, now seems to be the time. And with the clear current focus on standards, curriculum development, and students' needs, now is the time for IDM.

IS NUCLEAR POWER WORTH THE RISKS?

KAS Science Standards	**HS-PS1-8** Develop a model to illustrate the changes in the composition of the nucleus of the atom and the energy released during the process of fission, fusion, and radioactive decay. **PS1.C: Nuclear Processes** Nuclear processes, including fusion, fission, and radioactive decays of unstable nuclei, involve release or absorption of energy. The total number of neutrons plus protons does not change in any nuclear process. (HS-PS1-8) **Developing and Using Models** Develop a model based on evidence to illustrate the relationships between systems or between components of a system. (HS-PS1-8)
Staging the Compelling Question	After examining the map, "NRC Regions" and locations of nuclear reactors, use the Question Formulation Technique to generate questions about the locations of nuclear reactors.

Supporting Question 1	Supporting Question 2	Supporting Question 3	Supporting Question 4
How is nuclear fuel created?	How does the production and waste of nuclear fuel compare to coal and natural gas?	What are the external dangers of nuclear power?	What are the key government policies related to nuclear energy?
Formative Performance Task	**Formative Performance Task**	**Formative Performance Task**	**Formative Performance Task**
Create a graphic organizer describing how nuclear fuel is produced in relation to its half-life.	Write a paragraph that compares and contrasts the production and waste of nuclear fuel with the extraction and pollution of coal and natural gas.	Develop an evidence-based claim about the external dangers posed by nuclear power.	Develop an evidence-based claim that evaluates how well nuclear government policies provide for public safety.
Featured Sources	**Featured Sources**	**Featured Sources**	**Featured Sources**
Source A: NEI "Nuclear Fuel Process" explaining extraction **Source B:** Nuclear Fuel Fabrication: How ore is converted to fuel **Source C:** Nuclear Fuel Cycle explaining the full process with half-lives	**Source A:** NEI "Cost Benefit Analysis" **Source B:** European Nuclear Society "Fuel Comparison" **Source C:** Cost Comparison for Nuclear vs. Coal	**Source A:** Council on Foreign Relations "Targets for Terrorism: Nuclear Facilities" **Source B:** Terrorism and Nuclear Energy **Source C:** Fact sheet on Seismic Issues for Nuclear Power Plants **Source D:** National Center for Disaster Preparedness "Nuclear Power Plants and Earthquake Risk"	**Source A:** NEI "Nuclear Waste Management" **Source B:** CRS "Nuclear Power Plant Security and Vulnerabilities" **Source C:** CRS "Nuclear Energy Policy"

Summative Performance Task	**ARGUMENT** Is nuclear power worth the risk? Construct an argument (e.g., detailed outline, poster, essay) that addresses the compelling question using specific claims and relevant evidence from scientific sources while acknowledging competing views.
	EXTENSION Conduct a Socratic seminar that examines waste disposal for existing power plants and postulate possible alternatives.
Taking Informed Action	**UNDERSTAND** Research the effects of nuclear power plants on local communities.
	ASSESS Examine the positives and negatives of permitting a nuclear power plant to operate near your community.
	ACT Contact your local representative/senator or energy expert and invite them into your classroom to talk about how your community might be impacted by nuclear energy.

FIGURE 10.2: 6TH GRADE MATHEMATICS INQUIRY

WHAT'S THE BEST WAY TO BUY THAT PLAYSTATION?

CCSS-M Standard Connections	**CCSS-M GRADE 6 EXPRESSIONS AND EQUATIONS:** Use variables to represent two quantities in a real-world problem that change in relationship to one another; write an equation to express one quantity, thought of as the dependent variable, in terms of the other quantity, thought of as the independent variable. Analyze the relationship between the dependent and independent variables using graphs and tables, and relate these to the equation.
Staging the Compelling Question	Research the price of the latest Playstation video console system and estimate what the next version will cost. Assuming you can save up to $35/month, how long will it take you to save up for it? If the system were bought with a parent's credit card, predict/guess what the system will cost given that the minimum payment you have to make each month is $35.

Supporting Question 1	Supporting Question 2	Supporting Question 3	
Understand	Understand	Assess	
What would be the credit account balance after one month?	How could the credit model become more sophisticated?	How do factors such as interest rate or payment amount affect the time to zero balance?	
Formative Performance Task	Formative Performance Task	Formative Performance Task	Formative Performance Task
Break the problem into steps and show calculations for figuring out the account balance for the credit card after the first month.	Translate the original calculations to a spreadsheet where each column represents a step in the calculation. Use the drag/copy feature to repeat the process for additional months to determine how long it would take to pay off the Playstation.	Modify the model to allow payments to happen on a different day of the month or with a different interest rate. Include a graphical representation of months versus balance.	Replace hard coded values with values linked to a separate cell to test different scenarios by changing that value.
Featured Sources	Featured Sources	Featured Sources	Featured Sources
Source A: *How Is Credit Card Interest Calculated?* Article	**Source A:** *How Is Credit Card Interest Calculated?* Article	**Source A:** *How Is Credit Card Interest Calculated?* Article	**Source A:** *How Is Credit Card Interest Calculated?* Article

Summative Performance Task	**ARGUMENT** What's the best way to buy that Playstation? Construct and present an argument (e.g., infographic, essay) that addresses the compelling question using specific claims supported with data scenarios from the spreadsheet model.
	EXTENSION Develop a "credit-wise"proposal for purchasing the Playstation.

NOTES

1. K. Swan, J. Lee and S.G. Grant, *Inquiry Design Model: Building Inquiries in Social Studies* (Silver Spring, MD: National Council for the Social Studies and C3 Teachers, 2018).

2. S. Goldman and Z. Kabayadondo (Eds.), *Taking Design Thinking to School: How the Technology of Design Can Transform Teachers, Learners, and Classrooms* (New York: Taylor and Francis, 2016).

3. Holmes Group, *Tomorrow's Teachers: A Report of the Holmes Group* (East Lansing, MI: The Holmes Group, 1986).

4. Sam Wineburg and Daisy Martin, "Tampering with History: Adapting Primary Sources for Struggling Readers," *Social Education* 73, no. 5 (September 2009), 212-216.

5. S.G. Grant, K. Swan and J. Lee, *Inquiry-Based Practice in Social Studies Education: The Inquiry Design Model* (New York: Routledge and C3Teachers, 2017), x.

6. S.G. Grant, K. Swan and J. Lee, *op. cit.*

7. L. Darling-Hammond, G. Wilhoit, and L. Pittenger, "Accountability for College and Career Readiness: Developing a New Paradigm," *Education Policy Analysis Archives*, 22, no. 86 (2014). Available online at: https://epaa.asu.edu/ojs/article/view/1724

Conclusion

Our work on this book and in previous Inquiry Design Model (IDM) books has aimed to elevate inquiry as a regular practice in schools. Taking on this challenge has been an ongoing effort. We led the writing of the C3 Framework published in 2013 to provide guidance for state standards to support inquiry learning. We built the New York Toolkit in 2014 as a collection of inquiry-based materials to bring the C3 Framework to instructional life. We then generated a theory for inquiry in our first IDM book, *Inquiry-Based Practice in Social Studies Education: The Inquiry Design Model*.[1] Next, we developed an approach to designing inquiries in our second IDM book, *Building Inquiries in Social Studies: The Inquiry Design Model*.[2] Now, in this book, we have taken on the challenge of IDM curriculum. Our work is intended to provide educators with the structures and the language they need to speak "inquiry" fluently across a social studies course and throughout a school or district.

We have introduced lots of new ideas in this book—structured, embedded action, focused, guided, and self-directed inquiry blueprints, vertical and horizontal looping, IDM assessment systems, and IDM thinking. Along the way, we pushed the edges of our thinking about inquiry and IDM by talking not just about lessons or one-off implementation, but about curriculum. We aimed to do something new with this book and to write it as an exercise in thinking about the whole of inquiry education. So, what have we learned? We think four things rise to the top—inquiry design is dynamic, inquiry curriculum is more than the sum of its parts, we can do assessment through inquiry, and IDM is a way of thinking.

First, we learned that IDM is dynamic. When we conceived of IDM, we put our ideas in a box, literally! The blueprint is full of boxes. This sort of thinking was useful at the time. We wanted to create an approach to designing inquiry and products of those designs that were coherent and consistent. But, as is often the case, coherence and consistency can lead to predictability and inertia. The original blueprint—a compelling question, three supporting questions and tasks, pre-selected featured sources, and additional tasks—served an important purpose. It jumpstarted teachers' thinking about what inquiry could be and how to do it in their classrooms. However, that initial blueprint was not a be all and an end all. Almost from the beginning we found teachers pushing and pulling on the blueprint, eager to do it their way. Predictability gave way to innovation, and from then on new inquiry types began to emerge.

We were inspired by these innovative teachers, and the products of their innovations are represented here. The focused inquiry is a scaled-down version of the "Coke Classic" structured inquiry. Focused inquiry centers a concept, skill, or even a source that drives the inquiry in an efficient manner and helps teachers deal with the strain of content coverage. Guided, embedded action, and self-directed inquiries stretch out IDM even more by providing teachers and students with more room to roam, more autonomy, and more flexibility in how tasks interact with one another. Together these five inquiry types that have been discussed in this book represent our expanding ways of thinking about IDM, but they are not just five discrete approaches to designing individual inquiries. Curriculum matters too.

IDM and all of the inquiries that are designed and implemented using the new approaches suggested in this book and all those to be imagined going forward are more than just the sum of their parts. When thoughtfully organized and coordinated in a course or in a multi-grade program of study, inquiries become a curriculum. In this book, we have introduced the notion of curriculum looping to represent the idea that inquiries, when held together in thoughtful ways, can provide students with powerful opportunities to build their knowledge and to practice the skills needed to be successful in civic life. We have developed the notion of horizontal looping as a way to structure a series of inquiry-based experiences that recur and ratchet up over the course of a school year. Teachers may have students work on looping content and/or skills to build up their capacities. Teachers may even use different inquiry types when looping horizontally. Similarly, we have proposed the notion of vertical looping to represent ways in which inquiry design and implementation can be coordinated across courses and grades. When looping vertically, teachers are purposefully repeating inquiry experiences across a course of study. Taking on the big curriculum picture through the notion of looping is an essential aspect of bringing IDM into full relief in school. In this way, inquiry becomes more than a single-day or a one-week experience. But, that's easy stuff compared to what we learned next.

A big realization has been that teachers *can* do meaningful assessment through IDM. We have had some fits and starts along the way in coming to this realization. At times, assessment has seemed like the third rail of education. At other times, it has seemed like a sinkhole. Our work with assessment and inquiry has been (and continues to be) a journey. Along the way, we realized two very important things about assessment and IDM. First, the IDM blueprint is an assessment. Baked into the blueprint from the beginning is a means by which to systematically assess student learning. Formative tasks enable teachers to collect information about what students are learning along the way and provide critical feedback to move them forward. Summative assessment is a chance for teachers to gauge their students' competency, specifically their capacity to make an evidence-based argument. The second thing we realized is that the blueprint is more than just formative and summative assessment. As an assessment *system*, IDM has two interlocking parts. The first is the formative/summative structure that is so clearly evident in the blueprint. The second part of the IDM assessment system deals with the work students do after the summative argument. This second part of the IDM assessment system takes seriously those tasks of extension and taking informed action that breathe civic life into our inquiries.

From the new inquiry types, curriculum looping, and the IDM assessment system, we ultimately learned that IDM is a way of thinking, a way of thinking rooted in problem solving. We originally built IDM to solve a problem—the problem of how to bring the ideas in the C3 Framework to instructional life. With the general IDM theory in place, we went about the business of taking on new problems. In our second book, it was the problem of how to design an inquiry in a systematic manner. There we took on the challenge of growing IDM into new forms and representing these new inquiry types as curriculum with implications for assessment. IDM as a way of thinking also allows us to take on the challenge of coordinating IDM as an approach to inquiry among many approaches and to do so across the disciplines.

We have learned much in the journey of writing this book, but we can't help but ask, what's next? One thing we are sure of is that we will continue to listen to and learn from teachers. We know from our experiences writing this book that, when we listen to teachers and support their best intentions and efforts, new ideas, things we've not conceived of, are possible. So, what's next? Continuing to work closely with teachers to learn from their practices using inquiry in the classroom. We have some ideas for what that might involve. But we need to know more about how teachers manage instructional time when implementing inquiry. We have lots of new inquiry types introduced in this book (likely with more to come), but we also need to know about how teachers manage the implementation of tasks and sources and how they maximize students' efforts while reaching each student as individual learners. We need to know more about how teachers manage the content of an inquiry and how students interact with and learn that content. Just answering the simple question—"What are students learning about and how are they learning content through inquiry?—is an important next step. We need to know more about how teachers scaffold their students' learning and meet the diverse needs of students in the many contexts within which inquiry learning takes place. We need to know more about how we assess and, yes, grade inquiry. The systems are in place, so how do teachers implement those assessment systems? All of these questions and more are what we think will be the newest opportunities to push IDM forward. That's what's next, and that's what excites us most.

We created C3 Teachers (www.c3teachers.org) to take on all of these challenges and opportunities. C3 Teachers is a simple idea—bring together educators who are passionate about inquiry and want to know more. We did just that and it has certainly been useful. C3 Teachers is now a network of thousands of teachers who are accessing and sharing ideas about teaching with inquiry. In the first pages of this book, we said that inquiry is to education as liberty is to democracy—it's baked into the cake. Whether you are baking a cake or building an educational program, you need the ingredients for success. The ideas presented in this book offer some of those ingredients. The blueprint, various inquiry types, looping curriculum, inquiry assessment, IDM thinking--these are some of the ingredients needed to build a powerful educational program. With C3 Teachers in the lead, we will continue to bring all these new ingredients together, and find those that we might still be missing, so as to build the most effective system of inquiry-based education that is possible.

NOTES

1. S.G. Grant, K. Swan and J. Lee, *Inquiry-Based Practice in Social Studies Education: The Inquiry Design Model* (New York: Routledge and C3 Teachers, 2017).

2. K. Swan, J. Lee and S.G. Grant, *Inquiry Design Model: Building Inquiries in Social Studies* (Silver Spring, MD: National Council for the Social Studies and C3 Teachers, 2018).

About the authors

Kathy Swan is a professor of social studies education in the College of Education at the University of Kentucky.

S.G. Grant is a professor of social studies education in the Department of Teaching, Learning, and Educational Leadership at Binghamton University.

John Lee is a professor of social studies education in the College of Education at North Carolina State University.